P9-CFC-777

The Book of
Upholstery

The Book of
Upholstery

UNDERSTANDING AND
DECORATING
WITH UPHOLSTERED
FURNITURE

Candace Ord Manroe

CRESCENT
BOOKS
New York • Avenel

A FRIEDMAN GROUP BOOK

This 1997 edition is published by Crescent Books,
a division of Random House Value Publishing, Inc.
40 Engelhard Avenue, Avenel, New Jersey 07001

Crescent Books and colophon are trademarks of Random House Value Publishing, Inc.

Random House
New York • Toronto • London • Sydney • Auckland

Copyright ©1997 by Michael Friedman Publishing Group Inc.

All rights reserved. No part of this publication may be reproduced, stored in a retrieval system,
or transmitted, in any form or by any means, electronic, mechanical, photocopying, recording, or otherwise,
without prior written permission from the publisher.

ISBN 0-517-14272-4

THE BOOK OF UPHOLSTERY: Understanding and Decorating with Upholstered Furniture
was prepared and produced by Michael Friedman Publishing Group, Inc.
15 West 26th Street
New York, New York 10010

Editors: Tony Burgess and Celeste Sollod
Art Director: Kevin Ullrich
Photography Editors: Samantha Larrance and Wendy Missan
Production Manager: Camille Lee

Color separations by Fine Arts Repro House Co., Ltd.
Printed in Hong Kong by Wing King Tong Co Ltd.

10 9 8 7 6 5 4 3 2 1

DEDICATION

To my children,
Meagan, Drew, and Sam.

CONTENTS

INTRODUCTION

PURCHASING A NEW PIECE of upholstered furniture or having an older piece re-upholstered is one of the more expensive and challenging decisions that a modern consumer ever has to face. In the last century and earlier, before the Industrial Revolution, the process for the purchaser was still expensive, but at least it was simple. All you had to do was to find a reputable upholsterer and let him or her know your needs. Upholsterers all did basically the same thing, and the only question was how well they did it. But now, with a plethora of manufacturers offering a diverse spectrum of materials and processes, covering a broad range of price points, the choices are intimidatingly numerous. What once was a standard process employed by the master craftsman of old—the same process for each upholsterer—is increasingly a rarity, and one that bears a hefty price-tag, especially if it is to be performed well. Adding to the confusion is the fact that technological innovations are constantly adding to the menu of materials. Keeping up with all the new kinds of foams for stuffing, coil designs for springs, and fabrics for covers is a daunting and time-consuming task.

So what is a buyer to do? Short of spending years learning the art of upholstery yourself, there are two important ways to prepare yourself. First, gaining some basic knowledge of upholstery materials and techniques can remove much of the fear associated with making upholstery choices. By learning the vocabulary and some of the main options in the upholstered furniture industry, you, the consumer, will become able to ask the right questions to help you make a wise decision. Even

Selecting an upholstered furnishing or re-upholstering an old favorite can be a daunting process. What you need is some basic knowledge about fabrics and upholstering techniques, as well as a sense of your personal style.

Identifying your personal style is not as difficult as it sounds. Reflect on the things you like and balance that with the practical considerations of your lifestyle.

amid ever-changing technological advances, being armed with fundamental knowledge and sound questions is the best way to prepare yourself to make this difficult purchase.

The second ingredient for a successful purchase, and perhaps the more important and difficult, is to develop a clear sense of your own particular style and taste. Every good decorator knows that one of the hardest parts of his or her job is finding out what the client really wants. By taking the time to carefully consider the kinds of questions that a decora-

tor would ask, you can come to a much better understanding of your own tastes, needs, and desires, and you may be surprised by some of the things you discover.

This book is not intended to produce do-it-yourself furniture upholsterers. It is intended to produce smart, informed consumers of upholstered furniture. The goal is to make you confident enough in your choices that you will be truly satisfied with your purchase, enjoying years of contentment living with your upholstered furniture pieces.

Chapter

1

Opposite: This early illustration of a French upholsterer's shop depicts seamstresses carefully preparing the material that will be used to cover chairs.

Right: A swivel chair from The Hermitage, Andrew Jackson's home in Nashville, Tennessee. The beauty of this chair lies in its unadorned carving and fine craftsmanship.

IN THE HOME FURNISHINGS industry, where buzzwords come and go on a seasonal basis that mirrors the fickleness of fashion, two ubiquitous adjectives promise to go the distance: comfortable and casual. Both conjure images of soft, cushiony chairs and sofas that invite curling up on; fabrics with an eminently touchable feel that won't be the worse for wear; upholstery treatments that are user-friendly, adapting to the shape of the person sitting while still providing proper body support and near-sybaritic pleasure.

Given the emphasis on casual comfort, it's hard to imagine a time when hard, unupholstered wooden furniture was the only option in a home's decor. But from an historical standpoint, it wasn't all that long ago. As recently as the sixteenth century, textiles were used only in the wealthiest of households, and then primarily as draperies, wall hangings, and floor and bed coverings.

EARLY UPHOLSTERERS

TEXTILES DID NOT COME into use as furniture coverings until the early seventeenth century. Prior to then, the upholsterer, or "upholder," as he was called, was something of an interior designer/master craftsman, who not only installed but also hand-crafted all of the decorative treatments in the home that utilized textiles.

An exclusively male domain, the job of the early upholsterer was considered extremely prestigious. Upholsterers did not dress in workman's attire but in a gentleman's finery. One of the early London guilds, which was granted its coat of arms in 1465, bore the telling name The Worshipful Company of Upholders. Even when the onset of the seventeenth century meant that the job of upholsterer expanded to include what's now considered its primary focus, covering furniture, the extreme costliness of textiles meant that their use on furniture was restricted to royalty or the very rich. Commissioning an upholsterer to cover furnishings carried many of the same connotations then as hiring an interior designer does today, though fewer homeowners could afford the services.

Left: Once only royalty and the very rich could afford to cover furniture with textiles. This 1829 watercolor depicting the office of Prince Metternich in Vienna is evidence of his privilege.

Opposite: The prestige granted early upholsterers is reflected in this elaborate trade card for William Darby of London.

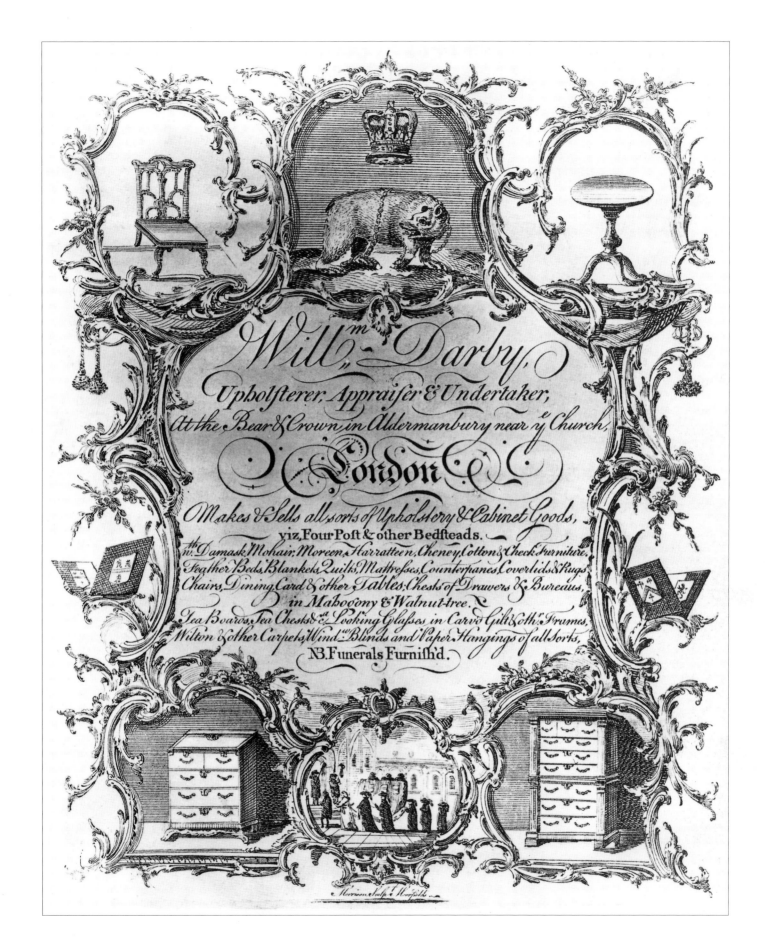

SEVENTEENTH-CENTURY
Upholstery

THE EARLIEST KNOWN examples of upholstered furnishings date back to 1610 in England. They featured flat, firmly stuffed cushions, known as squab cushions, on settees, chairs, and wooden storage chests that doubled as seating. The earliest covered pieces included the X chair, which got its name from wooden legs that formed an X in both front and back. These generally uncomfortable chairs featured simple, hard, upholstered seats with little ornamentation. The framework of the typical X chair was en-tirely covered in leather (or, less often, in more costly fabric). The covering was closely fastened with decorative brass nails that hid the tangent where the leather met the cross members. The seats were thick squabs, hardly comfortable by today's standards, filled with horsehair, lamb's wool, or even, in some cases, marsh grass. The squabs lay upon straps of leather or fabric stretched and nailed across the seat members. Chair backs were either narrow strips of leather or leather that was thinly upholstered across the two uprights.

Above: This reproduction of a Knole settee is covered in tapestry, and was designed with today's comfort standards in mind. The decorative ornaments at the back of the settee are a traditional detail.

Opposite: This distinctive example of the X chair (c. 1630) is an original now in the Victoria & Albert Museum in London. Covered in velvet, which was less common than leather, it features decorative brass nails that fasten the material to the frame.

Another seventeenth-century upholstered seating piece was the Knole settee, a precursor to the sofa. Though just as hard and uncomfortable as the X chair, the Knole settee was more elaborately ornamented with decorative textile trimmings. The Knole settee was shaped like a box with a high back and tall adjustable sides, both of which served the important function of providing protection from the inevitable drafts that blew through the poorly insulated dwellings. These settees were minimally upholstered with squab seats, but what they lacked in comfort, they made up for in ample decoration. The backs and seat squabs were ornamented with gold-thread braid. Deep fringes finished the bottoms, and the backs were sometimes decorated with draped pelmets trimmed in fringe. Pelmets were decorative cornice-like textile crowns used primarily to conceal the fixtures of curtains or drapes. Seventeenth-century upholders adapted them as ornaments at the top of the settee back. Both the X chair and the Knole settee are believed to have been constructed especially for a visit by James I to Knole House at Sevenoaks in Kent.

Only the very wealthy could afford to use fabric instead of more moderately priced leather for upholstered furniture. When fabric was used, it was usually a coarse needlework material known as turkeywork. In use since the beginning of the sixteenth century, turkeywork was designed to imitate the look and texture of oriental rugs, and was primarily used for floor and wall coverings. As English needleworkers stepped up production of the fabric in the seventeenth century, turkeywork quickly became the fabric of choice for upholstered furniture and other household coverings. So much turkeywork was produced during this period that extant pieces can still be viewed today in museum collections in both England and the United States.

In colonial America, foreign imports were extremely popular among the wealthy, and turkeywork-upholstered furniture was the ultimate status symbol. Other costly imported textiles, such as silks and damasks from France and Italy, brocades and velvets from Spain, and painted and printed chintzes from England and India, were also coveted as emblems

Left: In the seventeenth century, the needlework material
known as turkeywork was a
popular fabric for upholstering furniture. Needlework
is still valued for its rich,
textured look.

Below: This turkeywork chair,
which can be found in the
Victoria & Albert Museum
in London, originally had
a decorative fringe that
dangled from the seat and
back cushion.

of graciousness, although their use was restricted mainly to draperies, not furniture.

The 1691 household furniture inventory records of John Bowles' parlor in Roxbury, Massachusetts, in-cluded the following entries: thirteen chairs covered with leather, six chairs covered with turkeywork, and four needlework-covered stools. Uphol-stered stools were quite popular in England from about 1600 onward, and they caught on in the colonies from 1685 to 1720. Some extant museum pieces from that time are covered in a multicolored zigzag pattern known as flame stitch.

With the exception of the upholstered X chair and Knole settee, as well as a few other pieces that featured hammock-type suspension seating, furniture in the first half of the seventeenth century was constructed entirely of wood. Comfort in the home was not yet a priority among the general population. But as the century progressed, gradual concessions were made to comfort, and furniture designers began producing pieces with softer seats and backs. Cane or wood seating topped with tapestry- or velvet-covered cushions was introduced to temper the hardness of chairs and day beds. Similar to today's chaise lounge, the daybed was a simple wooden piece with a straight back and a long seat for stretching out the legs.

The original daybeds were covered only in a thin, tied-on cushion that barely gave the illusion of comfort.

During the William and Mary period, toward the end of the seventeenth century, more furniture was being upholstered, in a wider range of fabrics. These fabrics included Indian printed cotton (chintz), damasks, brocades, petit point embroidery, and crewel work, all of which were commonly dressed up even further with elaborate trimmings. By this time in North America, the rising middle class was fully engaged in the endless struggle to "keep up with the Joneses," and upholstered furnishings covered in any of the imported fabrics were prized possessions that proclaimed one's wealth and status.

Upholstered furnishings covered in rich, imported fabrics were coveted in the late seventeenth century. This elaborately carved daybed dates to 1695, and is covered in its original fabric from Genoa, Italy.

EIGHTEENTH-CENTURY
Upholstery

THE TURN OF THE EIGH-teenth century heralded the golden age of furniture. The furniture designs from the important English cabinetmakers, including Chippendale, Hepplewhite, and Sheraton, all emerged in the eighteenth century, and all remain classics in traditional design today. Although all of these designs are known primarily for their distinctive wood forms, they are also characterized by some important developments in upholstery techniques.

During the reign of Queen Anne, at the beginning of the eighteenth century, the first "stuffover" (what we now call overstuffed) upholstery appeared and, with it, a new form of chair: the now-classic wing chair (or easy chair, as it was then known). Like the Knole settee before it, the wing chair was designed with sides or "wings" intended to serve as a buffer from household drafts. The idea behind overstuffing, which then represented a new development in upholstering, is simple: instead of the interior upholstery stuffing being fitted between the parts of the frame of the chair (or any other seating piece), it is "top stuffed" over the surface of the seat members only, resting on suspensions stretched across the upper edges of the frame rails. As in the seventeenth century, the most commonly used stuffing materials were horsehair and lamb's wool.

While leather remained the most popular upholstery covering, finer furniture makers, such as Chippendale, Hepplewhite, and Sheraton, favored morocco, which is made from goatskin as opposed to cowhide. Considered more refined than cowhide, morocco also had certain drawbacks: a higher cost and more wastage, due to the smaller skin size. Not only was the initial material more costly than leather, but it also required greater care in use. The material's labor-intensiveness increased the

Left: In the eighteenth century, during the reign of Queen Anne, the wing chair was born. Still a classic today, this reproduction features the overstuffed sides, or "wings," that originally gave the wing chair its name.

Above: An original George II settee. Its distinctive shape and intricately carved mahogany legs suggest it is from St. Martin's Lane in London, the fashionable street where Thomas Chippendale had his shop.

costs of upholstering even further. Today, morocco is rarely used to cover furniture, having priced itself out of the market.

Another upholstery covering used during the period was haircloth, a cotton weave with horsehair woven into its weft. Haircloth was durable and much less expensive than other upholstery materials; however, be-cause of the horsehair content, the texture of the fabric was rough and scratchy to the touch. Haircloth can still be found today, although it is sel-dom used—especially when comfort is a priority.

During the eighteenth century, artisans began manufacturing furni-ture with detachable seats and backs. The seats and backs were upholstered separately in the construction of a chair, and haircloth was the often the fabric of choice. Because the upholstered seats and backs were detachable, upholsterers were free to use finer and more heavily embellished moldings for the edges of the furniture. These finer moldings, along with narrow gimps (a ribbon-like, braided fabric stiffened with wire) and ornamental brass nails, replaced the more fanciful textile-based trims and fringes found on late-seventeenth-century pieces.

Another advantage of the removable upholstered seats and backs was a decorator's delight: for an entirely different look, the upholstery could be changed according to the season or mood, without having to replace the entire furnishing. These pieces were the first to lend themselves easily to reupholstering. In so doing, they also presaged today's popular slipcovers, detachable coverings that fit over a furnishing without being permanently affixed.

Still, the cost to reupholster a furnishing as well as to build a piece from scratch remained out of the reach of many. Below is a typical bill for building a chair from scratch, invoiced to John Brown of Providence, Rhode Island, in 1764 by the Plunket Fleeson firm in Philadelphia. Tallied in pounds, shillings, and pence, the

A Louis XV chair painted white with parcel gilt highlighting the chair's soft curves. The stuffed upholstered back was more comfortable than the wood backs on English chairs of the period.

invoice can be used to get an idea of the price of upholstery materials during the eighteenth century.

To a Mahogany Easy Chair Frame
. . . .£2 5s.

To Bottoming 6 chairs
@ 5s. ea.: . . . .£1 10s. 10d.

To 11 Yds Harateen
@ 4s./Yd: . . . .£2 4s.

To 13 Yrds Canvas for thee Chair
@ £1 6s./Yd: £19

To 8 lbs Curled Hair
@ 1s. 10d./lb: . . . . .14s.

To girth & Tax: . . . . .7s.

To 3.5 lbs of Feather
@ 3s./lb: . . . . .10s. 6d.

To 1.5 Yds of Ticken
@ 3s. 6d./Yd: . . . . .5s. 3d.

To 18 Yds Silk Lace
@ 8d/Yd: . . . . .12s.

To Thread Silk & Cord: . . . . . .3s.

To a sett castors: . . . . .8s.

To making the Easy Chair:
. . . .£1 15s.

Total: £26 18s. 19d.

FOR AMERICAN CONSUMERS of upholstered furniture, eighteenth-century England still exerts power as the source of the most important influences on today's designs. During this period, England experienced a rash of productivity and creativity in furniture design and craftsmanship unlike any that had come before or that were (thus far, at least) to follow. Beginning with Thomas Chippendale and continuing chronologically to include brothers Robert and James Adam, A. Hepplewhite, and Thomas Sheraton, the time from around 1750 to the end of the century was fertile for original furniture designs conceived by these master cabinetmakers. Their creations, which were documented in books published by the cabinetmakers themselves (a trend started by Chippendale), emerged as classics—the standards by which all subsequent furnishings are judged.

To appreciate today's offerings, it helps to know at least something about their fine precursors from the 1700s. Though some contemporary furnishings at may first glance bear little relation to their English fore-

This mahogany riband-back chair features the exquisite carving that is a hallmark of Chippendale design.

bears, no furniture has surpassed the designs of the eighteenth century in perfection of proportion, line, construction, and ornamentation. Even though a contemporary, sink-down cushy sectional sofa looks worlds apart from the carved-leg, firmly upholstered seating of two centuries before, the exacting standards set by the early piece remain the best, most telling yardstick for judging quality today.

CHIPPENDALE

Like many innovators, Thomas Chippendale received scant recognition during his lifetime for his amazing genius or for the enduring effect he was to have on furniture design through the ages. But time yields justice. Chippendale, the cabinet-maker who kept shop on London's fashionable St. Martin's Lane, has been more than avenged. While all other period furnishings are designated by the reigning monarch of their time—Elizabethan, Jacobean, Queen Anne, or the French King Louis styles—the most famous designs from the great period of English furniture-making (from the mid- to late-1700s) are most often known by one man's name: Chippendale. Today, the name alone connotes an elevated aesthetic and a refined sensibility.

Chippendale came by his craft honestly. His father was a master carver much in demand among the British upper classes for his picture frames and mirrors. But beyond that, and the fact that he was born in Worcestershire, little is known of the younger and most famous Chippendale's personal life; what remains, instead, as a living testament are his furniture designs, which he thankfully had the foresight to assign to posterity through publication in book form.

The Gentleman and Cabinetmaker's Director, an illustrated, catalog-style collection of his work, was first printed in 1754. A second edition followed in 1759 and a third in 1762, the rapid succession of publication dates pointing to the public's clamor for and interest in fresh furniture designs and cabinetmaking. Chippendale's book marked the first significant effort of its kind, paving the way for similar documentaries of design by the other English cabinetmakers who followed in his wake.

Because classical architecture was considered the foundation of all the arts in Chippendale's time, the cabinetmaker devoted the beginning of his book to the five classical orders. But this was more lip service than genuine tribute. In fact, his work was criticized early on for its lack of reference to or respect for the classical orders. Instead of relying on the ancient Greek forms for inspiration, Chippendale magically blended a mix of French, Gothic, and Chinese designs into a new, eclectic look uniquely his own. The carving on each of Chippendale's designs was exquisite, eliminating

These two chairs (c. 1760) reflect Thomas Chippendale's interest in Chinese design. He combined elaborate carving with practical considerations like a broad back and ample seat.

---

the need for further ornamentation such as inlay or paintwork.

Shape was everything, especially in chairs, which Chippendale considered the most important pieces of furniture. While Chippendale's use of French (rococo ribbon) or Chinese (latticework and pierced frets) carved designs gave his chairs a sculptural quality, he combined these decorative carvings with

English practicalities—a broad back and roomy seat to accommodate women's hooped skirts. Even the chairs' claw and ball feet and bandy legs, though carved in the French manner, reflect earlier English design features that Chippendale seamlessly wove with other influences into a new hybrid. But unlike those that preceded them, Chippendale's chairs had nothing awkward and ungainly about them; instead, they were remarkable for the equally fine and delicate carving on their cabriole legs and frames as on their backs, and for the perfect proportions between the various elements. At the same time, the chairs, as with other Chippendale furnishings,

had an appearance of bold solidity that conveyed a sense of permanence and weight.

Chippendale called his upholstered ("stuffed") chairs French, whether the carvings on them were rococo or not. (That was because of the popularity of stuffed chairs in France.) Although extant Chippendale chairs rarely have their original upholstery, those that do sport their original fabric feature seats of worsted close-stitch in floral, geometric, or figurative motifs. Besides needlework, other upholstery materials either found or referred to on original Chippendale chairs include tapestry, damask, and Spanish leather, which were held in place by mouldings or rows of decorative brass nails.

In addition to chairs, Chippendale showed an appreciation for stuffed sofas (as opposed to the more popular hard-back settees of the day, which were stuffed only at the seat). These sofas featured both tight stuffed backs and tight seats (no loose cushions) for greater sitting comfort, with the carving confined to the sofa legs and frame. Even among today's plush, all-upholstered coil-spring sofas, the standards of upholstery neatness—of cleanness of line—found on the Chippendale sofa still apply, though now standards of comfort are far higher.

THE ADAM BROTHERS

Brothers Robert and James Adam are best remembered for their contributions to architecture, recorded in a 1773 edition and later publications of *Works in Architecture of Robert and James Adam, Esquires.* But in addition to drawings of building styles, the book featured no less than sixty-four plates of furnishings— interior design appointments conceived in the same style as the larger spaces they were to occupy.

For the Adam Brothers, detail in upholstery was as important as detail in carving. This gilded chair (c. 1780) is an oval-backed design that features an elegant cream fabric and small covered buttons.

Just as Chippendale played upon earlier furniture themes, re-arranging and altering them to suit his taste and develop a unique style (the simple, solid wood backs of Queen Anne chairs, for example,

became pierced—a study in positive and negative space—in Chippendale's hands), so did the Adams use Chippendale and other styles as a departure point. Whereas Chippendale lauded the five classical architectural orders as the foundation of all good design and then went on to do more or less as he pleased, orders or not, the Adam brothers took the orders seriously, but refined and downscaled them to a delicacy theretofore unseen. Unlike the bold, strong shapes of Chippendale, Adam designs are more intricate and seemingly fragile, relying on detail more than on dramatic silhouette.

Detail on upholstery was just as important as detailed carving, as evidenced by the drawings of Robert Adam. He included separate colored sketches for the pattern of the silk to be used on a chair back and seat—and even the small cushion on the chair arm was graced with a design all its own. A true jack-of-all-trades (as upholsterers in general were, at that time), he designed the needlework, as well as the furniture framework. This gave Adam pieces a pleasing cohesiveness, a uniformity of design in which all parts fit gracefully together. Though much of the furniture was carved in mahogany and then gilded, it was frequently painted in Wedgwood colors to match a room's plaster walls.

In this fine Hepplewhite chair featuring his trademark shield back, delicate carving and an airy design create a graceful silhouette.

A. HEPPLEWHITE

Another standout talent of the eighteenth century is cabinetmaker A. Hepplewhite, whose works are documented in the 1788 publication *The Cabinet-Maker and Upholsterer's Guide*. The three hundred furnishings featured in this publication constitute one of England's most important contributions to the art of furniture making. Hepplewhite lacked Chippendale's inventive spirit and unerring eye for proportion, and his arrangement of ornamentation is

not as deft as Sheraton's, but his work is nonetheless valuable for its lightness of form and its unassuming grace.

On chairs, Hepplewhite's distinguishing trademark was the shield or heart-shaped back. This motif was present in his designs whether the legs were straight or curved. Within the shield, he included another signature—the wheat-ear or inverted bellflower, which became almost as well known as Chippendale's ribbon back or Sheraton's characteristic lyre. Hepplewhite's chairs were smaller than Chippendale's both in height and width, and their legs were thinner, more tapered versions of Chippendale's square, Chinese-inspired versions. The result appeared almost too fragile to support the seat, but thanks to a spade foot, the chairs were much stronger than they looked. A final trait of many Hepplewhite stuffed-seat chairs was their ornamentation with japanning—a hard, brilliant varnish—on the chair backs for a rich, finished look.

Like Chippendale, Hepplewhite took an interest in designing the newly popular stuffed-back chair. Unlike Chippendale, who called these chair types French, Hepplewhite termed his "cabriole"—a term that's confusing today, as it has come to refer to a turned leg. But Hepplewhite's cabriole chairs had both straight and turned legs. They were the height of fashion, commissioned by none other than the Prince of Wales. For the bedrooms of the wealthy, Hepplewhite designed the popular easy chair, known today as the wing-back chair for its protruding sides or wings. Hepplewhite, however, termed his easy chairs "saddle-check" chairs. Typically, they were upholstered in the same material found on the bed and at the windows.

THOMAS SHERATON

The last of the eighteenth-century cabinetmakers, Thomas Sheraton attained a reputation second only to Chippendale's as a master of aesthetics in furniture design. A stickler for detail, he was especially picky about every aspect of furniture mak-

Thomas Sheraton's designs are fragile in appearance only. The legs of this chair taper delicately toward the foot, yet it has survived nearly two centuries intact.

---

ing, from the selection of the wood to how it was crafted, as as is evident in his 1791 publication, *The Cabinet-maker and Upholsterer's Drawing-Book*. He raged against the absence of adequate instruction among his colleagues regarding perspective—an appreciation for geometry that he believed to be central to sound furniture.

Unlike Chippendale's, Sheraton's designs have a fragile appearance, yet they have withstood the passage of time amazingly well without falling into disrepair. This soundness is explained by Sheraton's minute instructions to craftsmen, in which he left nothing to guesswork, expressly directing each step of the process. His chair and sofa legs taper delicately toward the

foot. The trademark for which he is possibly best known is the lyre motif, which he often executed with inlays. Regrettably, some of his lyre-back chairs, however beautiful, are ergonomic failures by today's standards, forcing the body into an unhappily upright position from which leaning back even a bit is impossible.

Sheraton's stuffed-back upholstered (or "drawing room") chairs are more comfortable than the lyre-backs, but they lack originality of design. For the most part, they are duplications of the French form. As his career progressed, Sheraton borrowed more and more heavily from the French, his designs losing virtually all traces of English influence. Marquetry became important to his work, even more so than carving.

THE
CABINET-MAKER
AND
UPHOLSTERER's GUIDE;
OR,
REPOSITORY OF DESIGNS
FOR EVERY ARTICLE OF
HOUSEHOLD FURNITURE,
IN THE NEWEST AND MOST APPROVED TASTE:
DISPLAYING
A GREAT VARIETY OF PATTERNS FOR

Chairs	Tea Caddies	Hanging Shelves
Stools	Tea Trays	Fire Screens
Sofas	Card Tables	Beds
Confidante	Pier Tables	Field Beds
Ducheffe	Pembroke Tables	Sweep Tops for Ditto
Side Boards	Tambour Tables	Bed Pillars
Pedeftals and Vafes	Dreffing Glaffes	Candle Stands
Cellerets	Dreffing Tables and Drawers	Lamps
Knife-Cafes	Commodes	Pier Glaffes
Defk and Book-Cafes	Rudd's Table	Terms for Bufts
Secretary and Book Cafes	Bidets	Cornices for Library
Library Cafes	Night Tables	Cafes, Wardrobes, &c. at large
Library Tables	Bafon Stands	Ornamented Tops for Pier
Reading Defks	Wardrobes	Tables, Pembroke Tables,
Chefts of Drawers	Pot Cupboards	Commodes, &c. &c.
Urn Stands	Brackets	

In the PLAINEST and moft ENRICHED STYLES; with a SCALE to each, and an EXPLANATION in LETTER PRESS.

ALSO
THE PLAN OF A ROOM,
SHEWING THE PROPER DISTRIBUTION OF THE FURNITURE.

The Whole exhibiting near THREE HUNDRED different DESIGNS, engraved on ONE HUNDRED and TWENTY-EIGHT PLATES:

FROM DRAWINGS
By A. HEPPLEWHITE and Co. CABINET-MAKERS.

THE THIRD EDITION, IMPROVED.

LONDON:
Publifhed by I. and J. TAYLOR, at the ARCHITECTURAL LIBRARY, No. 56, HOLBORN, oppofite GREAT TURN-STILE.
MDCCXCIV.

Fabrics featuring patterns, like this grapevine, were not common until the nineteenth century, when woven textiles became less expensive to produce.

Opposite: An early advertisement for The Cabinet-Maker and Upholsterer's Guide. This third edition, published in London in 1794, features drawings by A. Hepplewhite and Co.

NINETEENTH-CENTURY
Upholstery

DEVELOPMENTS IN TECHnology led to major changes in furniture upholstery during the nineteenth century. The two most important developments that forever changed upholstery treatments were the invention of the Jacquard loom in 1803 and the introduction of coil springs in 1828. The Jacquard loom made woven fabrics much easier to produce and significantly less expensive. As a result, furniture upholstered in fabric was much more accessible to a larger number of people than it had ever been before. Coil springs, in turn, made seat cushions deeper and much more comfortable. Suddenly, upholstered furniture was much more available and utilitarian than it had ever been before.

Like so many inroads in the name of progress, coil springs did not entail entirely positive consequences. During the Victorian era, master craftsmen and those with keen aesthetic sensibilities lamented the decline of the finely crafted look in upholstered furniture. Coil-sprung furnishings tended to be much bulkier, and did not have the fine trimmings and ornamental touches of earlier classical furniture styles.

Left: The Jacquard loom, invented in 1803, made it easier and less expensive to produce woven fabrics. This helped popularize upholstered furniture.

Below: Early Victorian rosewood armchairs with heavy ornate legs. Although the introduction of coil springs in 1828 made seat cushions more comfortable, many disliked the bulkier furniture that followed this invention.

More decorative than functional, this elaborate daybed features Regency brass-inlaid mahogany and ebony. Four gilded rams decorate the legs.

Coil springs, however, were not solely responsible for the decline in upholstery craftsmanship. Many Victorian pieces featured poorly constructed frameworks with low-quality fillings such as woodwool (wood shavings) and shoddy (rag flock). Another popular, but inferior, filling of the period was alva, a dried seaweed used as a first stuffing, topped with cotton flock as the final or second filling. None of these filling materials was very durable, rendering salvage of many Victorian furnishings not worthwhile unless the pieces are entirely reupholstered.

The technological advances impairing craftsmanship did have one saving grace: they spawned a rebellion. In England, Scotland, and the United States—which was the center of the Arts and Crafts Movement—artisans led a return to the fine principles of quality materials and superior craftsmanship in the construction of furnishings and other decorative household items.

Especially in the early Victorian era, when coil springs were not yet widely employed, furnishings were constructed using primitive filling techniques, resulting in seated pieces that lacked spring or bounce. But with a thought to comfort, craftsmen compensated by increasing the amount of upholstery filling, for a softer seat. By today's standards, though, most of these pieces do not compare in terms of comfort. With their tight-back seats and backs, or

*Inspired by Victorian tastes
for fancy fabrics and trims,
this inviting windowseat
abounds with fringed pillows
and braided cushions.*

tufted treatments, the upholstered pieces seem distinctly stiff and rigid, contributing to Victorian furniture's reputation as more decorative than functional.

Many of the Victorian upholstered furnishings that commonly graced the well-appointed parlor are now obsolete. The meridienne (a type of settee-sofa with a sculptural shape), curule stool, gondola chair, and window bench—de rigueur in Victorian rooms—are seldom fixtures in today's homes. Opulent Victorian upholstery fabrics and trims, such as crimson silk, linen, and wool blends with gold medallions woven into the fabric, and showy braids and fringes are not used today except in the most formal interiors. Fancier trims are experiencing a revival today, but coupled with more practical main upholstery fabrics to create comfortable contemporary seating.

THROUGHOUT THE TWEN-tieth century, many furniture styles have gone in and out of vogue. However, almost regardless of style, some basic trends for upholstered furniture that were developed in the 1900s are still with us. Emphasis has been placed on upholstered pieces that are comfortable to sit or stretch out on, that will retain their shape and offer longevity, and that are compatible with real-life wear and tear. Hands-off showpieces still have a place in the home, but usually as stellar wooden or metal furnishings, not as upholstered seating pieces. Even in the most formal living rooms, comfort and practicality are still concerns for upholstered furnishings.

Earlier in the century, though, when the modern movement developed, sink-down upholstered comfort wasn't the top priority among the architects responsible for furniture designs now recognized as modern classics. Just as the Arts and Crafts Movement in the late 1800s was a rebellion against the mass-production and ornamental excesses of Victoriana, a generation of architects following close in the Craftsman-style footsteps rebelled by embracing new alternatives in building materials and

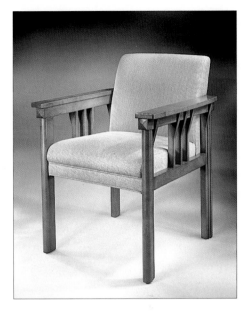

techniques for the construction of furniture. Their whole intent was to create fine designs that could be mass produced.

This meant exploring man-made building materials, both for furniture frames and for upholstery fillings and fabrics. In most cases, it also meant emphasizing the frame of the furniture over its upholstery. Many of the contemporary classics aren't upholstered at all. When they are, the upholstery is only a thin covering, little more than a skin that emphasizes the furnishing's pure, almost sculptural furnishing silhouette.

To illustrate, there is Marcel Breuer's famous Cesca armchair (1928), made of a bent steel tubing frame with seat and back covered in

The simple design of this chair is representative of the Arts and Crafts Movement, which emerged, in part, in opposition to the ornamental excesses of Victorian furniture.

stretched cane. The chair is clean and relatively comfortable, but without a shred of the filled upholstery usually associated with a soft seat. Later in the century there were the contemporary classics of Charles Eames, whose experiments with molded plywood, fiberglass, and light metal during the 1940s, 1950s, and 1960s resulted in thinly upholstered cushions filled with urethane foam enclosed by polyester fiber batting. On these pieces the cushions were something of an afterthought, not the most essential factor in the seating's character.

Working at about the same time, Eero Saarinen, son of the famous Finnish architect Eliel Saarinen, gained fame in 1948 with his easy chair, better known as the "womb" chair. Produced by Knoll with a steel rod base and polished chrome finish, the womb chair's upholstery included

foam over a molded plastic shell—another tight upholstery treatment with only the thinnest of profiles.

In between these contemporary architects/furniture designers came Ludwig Mies van der Rohe, master of the modern movement and father of the "less is more" school of design. Appointed director of the Bauhaus — a school of architecture noted for its synthesis of technology, craftsmanship, and design—in 1930, only to close the school three years later as a protest against Nazism, the German-born designer is best known for his Barcelona chair (1929). Produced by Knoll International, it features a pol-

Left: A Breuer chair designed for the Bauhaus in 1924 with simple linen stretched across the seat and back.

Below: A 1920s Marcel Breuer club chair known as the Wassily Chair. By design, the sculptural quality of the chair is emphasized over the upholstery.

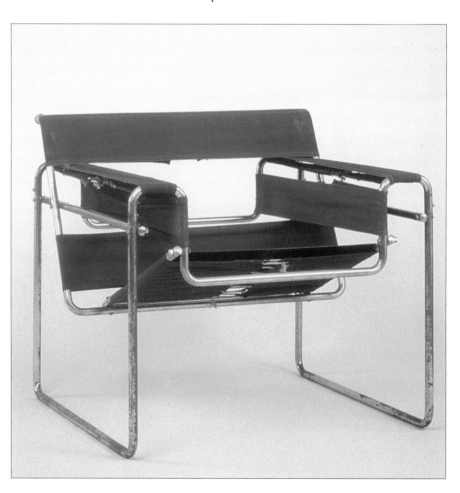

*The Barcelona chair,
designed by Ludwig Mies
van der Rohe, the master
of the modernist movement.
First produced by Knoll
International in 1929,
this chair features a
stainless steel frame and
leather cushions.*

ished, stainless steel frame and a foam mattress with polyester fiber padding covered in leather. Made without springs, the Barcelona chair, like other contemporary classics, offers firm seating, but not plush comfort. The modern pieces, especially early productions from the original factories (knock-offs are common), are considered collectibles today, meriting an important place in the home or office, but, again, not as the designated seats of comfort.

But more than any previous era, the twentieth century is not dominated by any single school of design. At the same time that the most renowned architect/furniture designers were exploring new materials and forms in a modern or minimalist vein, other furniture designers were doing some experimenting of their own. In the 1930s, this meant the emergence

of the first modular seating units as a result of the Art Deco style. These pieces reappeared in the 1970s, when Deco underwent a revival. Thick and deep, the modular seating groups typically featured a polyfoam filling over a wood frame, for an all-upholstered piece. They offered the same clean look that is a hallmark of contemporary styling, but with a more heavily cushioned profile than the architectural furnishings.

Along with the movement toward streamlined design came a reciprocal movement toward cleaner-looking textiles. Simplicity was the key. Since the 1950s, the movement toward texture over printed pattern has gained strength. Weaves in white or other neutral colors have patterns actually woven into the fabric, eliminating the need for a printed design. While this trend toward a more Spartan sensibility in textiles enjoys its largest audience among practitioners of contemporary design, it also has worked its way into country, traditional, and transitional interior designs, not eliminating printed textiles, but offering a clean counterpoint, even if only on an accent piece or a single furnishing, such as the sofa.

Beginning in the late 1970s, with the emergence in the United States of two national design magazines devoted exclusively to country style, country design became the major contender in home decorating. In all of its many variations, from country French to primitive American country, with dressier country English and cottage country in categories of their own, country design has left an impact on home furnishings in general. With its emphasis on casual comfort, the country school of design has influenced other furniture styles, which have gone to deeper seating and more wearable upholstery fabrics as a result. This means most upholstered furniture manufacturers now pride themselves on comfortable and long-lasting fillings and overall quality of construction.

No matter what the furniture style, mid-price-point upholstered pieces typically are made with tied coil springs or double-cone coils for plenty of support, no sag, spring action, and durability; and cushions

filled with high-density or HR (high resiliency) foam core wrapped in a

Left: Contemporary classics like this chair offer firm seating and style appropriate for both the home and office.

Below: The allure of the English country look is seen in the flowery charm of this room. The floral sofa and colorful screen are broken up by the solid fabric used for the chair.

Casual comfort plays an important role in home design today. This sofa's cushions are filled with down instead of foam for extra thickness.

synthetic covering such as Dacron. Down is often used as a sofa cushion filling when plush comfort is desired, but many designers and homeowners alike prefer foam instead of down to avoid the refluffing maintenance that

is necessary with sink-down down. Thicker, rolled arms, another practical concession to today's quest for comfort, are appearing on more sofas and chairs, resulting in fully upholstered pieces over hardwood frames.

Chapter

2

THE ART OF UPHOLSTERY

*This Art Deco–inspired chair
is covered in a neutral fabric
to preserve the emphasis on
its wonderful lines. The result
is understated elegance.*

RECALL THE OLD ADAGE that a little bit of knowledge can be a dangerous thing when reading this chapter. The nuts and bolts of upholstery techniques discussed in this chapter are not intended to instruct or prepare readers for complicated, or even simple, do-it-yourself upholstery projects. At the most, they may inspire such undertakings for a future date, but even that is not the real goal here.

Upholstered furniture is seen in every room of the home today. These dining chairs are a comfortable alternative to wood, and they complement the clean, contemporary design of this home.

Instead, this chapter is meant to impart a hands-on familiarity with some upholstery concepts in an effort to make consumers wiser when considering having a furnishing reupholstered or when purchasing new upholstered furniture. The basic idea is this: unless you are knowledgeable about how upholstered furniture is produced, you cannot possibly ask the right questions or provide the right description of your needs when dealing with a furniture upholsterer

or salesperson. The more you know about the materials, styles, and techniques of upholstery, the better equipped you will be to make wise choices. The following information is intended to remove all excuses for bad decisions based on insufficient knowledge; it is not intended to produce fledgling upholsterers. For more information on various upholstering projects you can pursue on your own, consult the Suggested Reading source list at the back of the book.

PRODUCTION

THROUGH THE FIRST FEW decades of this century, upholstering remained a craft pursued primarily by journeyed artisans who had paid their dues with years of appren- ticeship before striking out on their own as full-fledged upholsterers. Work was done entirely by hand using the traditional tools: needle and thread, tacks, hammer, and shears,

This wing chair is almost ready for its tapestry. Before foam rubber, natural materials such as horsehair were used as filling. Preparing and applying the stuffing was a very time-consuming process.

Upholstering is a simpler process than it was at the beginning of the twentieth century. Today, more people include more upholstered furnishings in their homes. This room alone has an upholstered sofa, chair, and ottoman.

plus a number of more specialized gadgets. Traditional upholsterers used a variety of natural filling materials, such as horsehair, palm fiber, moss, burlap, cotton, and muslin, employing techniques that were complicated and time-consuming. With the advent of foam rubber and all its derivatives, upholstering has become

a much more simplified process. Foam fillings have all but eliminated the most complicated part of traditional upholstering—the preparation, application, and regulation of the stuffing materials. Yet some current artisans still create upholstered furniture pieces using the old-school conventional stuffing materials and

techniques. These pieces, although sometimes less durable than foam-filled upholstery, tend to be more aesthetically pleasing and of a much higher quality. This hand-made craftsmanship, however, also means a much higher price tag. Even so, the old-fashioned filling techniques are well worth the extra effort and expense, especially when reupholstering an antique piece of furniture, because they help retain the natural lines and feel of the piece.

The goal of most modern furniture manufacturers facing upholstery jobs today is simple: to make the upholstery process as far as possible an efficient mass-production process; increased volume and reduced production time mean less cost and more profits. While this sounds like a cold, business-only attitude, most furniture manufacturers rely on their reputation for quality for repeat business and survival in the highly competitive industry. This means that they can't afford to compromise on quality. If the companies are to survive, they must produce attractive and functional upholstered furniture and sell it at a reasonable price in order to keep their customers happy. It is to the credit of the major manufacturers that their materials and techniques take into account comfort, lifestyle, and longevity. Unlike the auto industry, planned obsolesence isn't an ob-

vious part of the game plan. And while the newer products used in upholstering have lent themselves to mass-production, they have also had a direct consumer benefit. New techniques, materials, and styles have led to furniture construction that takes into account the human form, shaping the furniture to fit—and fit well—with proper body support where needed. Ergonomically correct furnishings illustrate progress at its best, facilitating good health without residual injury to society at large or to the environment.

Despite mass production methods, many manufacturers produce quality furniture that is both durable and comfortable. This overstuffed chair covered in vintage fabrics is stylish as well.

STAGES OF UPHOLSTERING

There are four elements to any upholstered piece: frame, springs, padding, and covering. The frame of this chair is responsible for its unique shape. We'll be following the reupholstering of this chair throughout the book

THE UPHOLSTERY PROCESS can be broken up into four distinct stages: the frame, the springs, the stuffing, and the fabric. By carefully looking at each of these stages you will gain a better understanding of how an upholstered piece is put together as well as what to look for when buying a new piece or getting an old one reupholstered.

FRAME

While the construction of the frame itself does not involve upholstering, building it is considered the first step in upholstering a furnishing because the frame must be completed before the actual covering work can begin. The frame constitutes the bones of the furnishing, the form that gives the piece its shape and substance before the upholstery is applied. How the frame is finished is determined by the type of upholstery that is to be used and where on the furniture the upholstery will be applied. Wood framing members that are to be covered are left raw and unfinished, while those that are to be exposed for viewing, without upholstery, are usually polished and finished.

Exposed wood areas give a good indication of the overall quality of a piece of upholstered furntiture. If the exposed arm or leg is of a high-quality hardwood, with a fine finish, then you can be fairly confident about the overall craftsmanship of the piece. The type of wood used is another good indicator of a piece of furniture's quality. Quality pieces are constructed with kiln-dried hardwood framing—the most popular choice being oak, with poplar and cottonwood

running a close second and third, respectively. Kiln drying, as opposed to air-drying, makes for more durable wood. Many low-end manufacturers cut corners by using plywood or particle board in their framing instead of hardwood. While this will cut the cost of a piece of furniture, it is not worth it in the long run, because you will be in the position of having to replace the chair or sofa much sooner than if you had spent the extra money for a piece made with quality wood.

SPRINGS

A wide range of springing is used in upholstering—from coil and no-sag springs to rubber straps and webbing. The type of springing used in upholstering depends upon the level of elasticity desired for the particular seat. There is also a wide variety in cost and complexity of production among the various spring types.

Rubber straps are often used for upholstering lounge (easy) chairs, but they can also be used for virtually any other type of upholstered seating. The quality of the chair's upholstering is determined, in part, by how the straps are attached and, equally important, by the number of straps used. If the straps are not attached correctly, the seat won't last—and the upholstering covering itself is rendered a moot point. At the same time

the more straps the craftsperson uses, the more secure the seating will be.

All open-framed seating requires webbing before covering. For nearly all dining chairs and other pull-up chairs, webbing is used, because rubber straps and light coil springs would make the seats too soft and too costly. The webbing is critical in these types of chairs as it forms the foundation for the upholstery. This is not an area in which quality can be compromised; should the webbing fall out of place, the entire furnishing will be ruined and must be reupholstered. All webbing should be made from top-grade jute (a strong burlap), sturdy

The frame and springs of the chair pictured on the previous page. The construction of the frame is considered the first step in upholstering furniture, even though it doesn't involve fabric.

nylon, or leather. The webbing should be folded at the end for extra strength and then tacked to the furniture frame with high-quality upholstering tacks. Webbing strips are applied from the front to the back of the seat, and they are crossbanded from one side to the other to create a platform for the remainder of the upholstery treatment. Stuffing material such as foam rubber or cotton padding is then placed over the webbing platform. Before the application of stuffing, the seat resembles a Shaker-style chair, whose over-and-under webbing is the actual outer seating material you can see on the unfurnished piece.

Strong webbing is essential to the durability of a chair. It should be made from top-grade jute, nylon, or leather.

No-sag springs are the most common choice for mass-produced upholstery. These are made from continuous wire shaped in a zigzag. This type of construction requires less time than other types of coil springs and is therefore less costly.

More expensive high-end furnishings employ double-cone coil springs. This is the best quality—and most expensive—spring for sofas and large chairs because it provdes a deep, comfortable, and resilient seat. Double-cone coil springs are made of heavy coiled metal that is shaped like an hourglass—larger at either end and tapering off at the middle. The size of the center coil determines the compression of the spring—hard, medium, or soft. The wider the center, the softer the seat.

Single cone springs differ from double cone springs in that they taper down from a large top coil to a narrower base coil. This type of construction tends to give less support than the double-cone springs.

The upholstered furnishing's quality is determined by the grade, number, and size of the springs, as well as by how they are arranged over the seat. Two methods are commonly used to mount coil and no-sag springs. On a rigid-edged seat, the springs are tied directly on top of the seat frame. On the spring-edge seat, the mounting allows the springs to move freely above the rail. Spring-edged seating indicates higher quality because it results in a more comfortable seat; however it is also more time-consuming to produce and, as a result, more expensive.

Top-of-the-line upholstered furnishings feature eight-way hand-tied coil spring construction. In this type of construction the coil springs are held in place by an interlocking web of cords made of high-quality material, such as Italian jute or imported hemp, fastened in eight hand-tied knots. This tying method ensures that the springs lie smooth across the furnishing. The high number of knots also means that if one rope of webbing should break, there are still six knots holding the piece in place. Four-way knots are adequate, but they won't provide the furniture with the longevity offered by eight-way knots.

Mid-price-point furnishings use a drop-in suspension method for eight-way hand-tied coil spring units. In this method, the coils are pre-tied and the entire suspension system is assembled in advance to fit a standard chair or sofa size. Pre-tied, drop-in coil units are typically tied with Number 9 wire, instead of webbing, and are therefore much less durable because wire has less flexibility than webbing. However, pre-tied coil spring units are a good option for the budget-minded consumer.

STUFFING

Today's expensive, high-quality upholstered seating pieces usually feature foam rubber as the padding material. For mass-produced lines with more accessible price points (the kind of furniture most consumers purchase), the soft filler is typically a type of polyurethane foam that is produced under a variety of names, such as polyfoam or latex foam. A combination of polyurethane and liquid foam rubber, which can be molded into the desired shape, is also used on mass-produced upholstery pieces. Quite often on reupholstery jobs where cotton was the original

Double-cone coil springs with eight-way knots provide the most comfortable and resilient seat. The wider the center coil, the softer the seat.

padding, the upholsterer will replace the natural filling with Dacron (on higher-quality furnishings) or polyester fiber (on the less expensive pieces). These newer products have made the early stuffing choices—horsehair, palm fiber, moss, burlap, cotton, and muslin—all but obsolete, except in custom upholstering jobs such as the reupholstery or exact reproduction of antiques.

The latest type of cushion filling to sweep the upholstery industry is high resiliency, or HR, foam. This is a type of polyurethane foam designed to keep its shape with heavy use and over long periods of time. It has an amazing resiliency and an uncanny ability to regain its shape after use.

Cotton was an early choice for padding. Today, many upholsters will replace a natural filling with man-made stuffing when reupholstering an antique.

The foam is available in varying compression factors (which indicates the amount of air pumped into the foam and how firm the cushion will feel) with a compression factor of 30 being the industry standard.

FABRIC

The fabric is the most important and the most expensive element in furniture upholstery. It is the one ingredient that can make or break not only the aesthetic appeal of a piece of furniture, but that of an entire room as well. The choice of fabric is also extremely important to the durability and functionality of the furniture. Whether it is a matter of purchasing a new seating piece that is already fabric-covered or having an existing furnishing reupholstered, the type and appearance of upholstery fabric determines the furnishing's functional and decorative success. Just because a fabric looks good, blending ideally with a room's palette and design style, does not guarantee that it is the best choice for that particular situation. Other factors, such as how the furnishing is going to be used and where it is to be positioned in the room, must be carefully considered when choosing an upholstery fabric.

If a sofa or a chair is to be the primary seating piece in a frequently used family room, the upholstery

When selecting upholstery fabric, it is important to consider how a piece of furniture will be used. This love seat is the primary seating piece in the room, so a comfortable, durable cotton fabric was selected to cover it.

fabric must be reasonably durable and comfortable to the touch. Fabric on heavily used furniture should never be purchased soley for show. It requires a material that you can sit back and relax on, without worrying about whether or not you will dirty or damage the fabric. On the other hand, upholstered furnishings in a formal living room that is used only on special occasions can incorporate more fragile, high-maintenance coverings, such as silk or linen, without creating any real problems.

Take into account the makeup of your family when selecting a fabric covering. If you have pets or young children who are prone to frequent spills, you will want to choose a dirt-resistant fabric—one that is easily cleaned in a color or pattern that does not readily show dirt and stains—such as cotton or perhaps a cotton-polyester blend. For durability, the fabric yarns should be closely woven and tightly twisted, much like those in the better-grade oriental rugs. A sturdy, tight weave (versus a loop pile or raised threads) is preferable for a household with pets, as is a color that will blend with the animal's hair, not showing every trace of inevitable

Above: This fabric was inspired by the rich carpet designs of the Middle East. This sort of heavy woven fabric is very durable.

rubberized backing. This type of backing is used to conceal the fact that there is a lower thread count per square inch in the weave, and means that the fabric is less durable than a full-weave fabric.

In addition to taking into account how and how often a piece of furniture will be used, its location within the room should also be determined before deciding upon a fabric. Does the room have a sunny exposure? Will the furnishing be placed close to a window, where harsh sun rays will take their toll? If so, avoid colorful fabrics made from materials such as silk or silk blends that are prone to

shedding. As a rule, more heavily woven fabrics are more durable. However, when buying a new piece, be sure that the fabric does not have a

Right: Consider where an upholstered piece will be positioned in a room. The dark fabric on this piece may become faded by the sunlight shining through the window above it.

fading and deterioration. Instead of a favorite, colorful print, consider a more neutral weave that won't fade. Will the seating piece be pulled close to the fireplace? If so, be sure the fabric selection is heat-resistant, and that the color is dark enough that it won't be ruined by smoke. Certain man-made fibers, such as polyester, acrylic, and acetate, are very heat sensitive in their pure form. Blended with a natural fiber, such as cotton, however, even these artificial fibers can be used in moderate-heat areas.

The general room temperature should be taken into account as well as extreme temperature considerations, such as a fireplace or a radiator. Even with climate control, some rooms are draftier than others in winter, while others are hotter in summer. For a room that's on the cool side in winter, you should avoid slick, shiny fabrics, which will enhance the chill. A better choice would be a sturdy wool blend or woven tapestry fabric, which will provide a welcoming warmth on a cold winter day. On the other hand, for a room that's unpleasantly warm in summer, a slick fabric covering that feels cool to the touch will be more inviting on a chair or sofa than a coarser textile in a nubby weave.

Answering these simple, practical questions regarding the furniture's use and placement should narrow the

range of acceptable fabric types. Once the practicality and durability considerations are determined, you must next decide on the aesthetics of the material—the palette, print, texture, and textile material, all of which contribute to achieving a desired look, mood, and decorating style. Aesthetic considerations will be covered more thoroughly in Chapter Four, "A Matter of Style." In order to get to that point, however, it is important to have a working knowledge of the

Above: Spend some time thinking about the mood and climate of a room before selecting fabric. The warm colors and plush sofa in this room invite you to curl up and relax.

Opposite: A simple diamond motif unifies this room. The chairs and the walls feature the same diamond shape.

types of textiles available as upholstery coverings in order to determine which ones are viable on a utilitarian level for your specific needs. Only then can a further investigation for decorative needs be intelligently carried out.

Fabrics can be broken into three general categories: those made from natural fibers (cotton, silk, linen, and wool); those made from man-made and synthetic fibers (polyester, nylon, acrylics, rayon, acetate, viscose rayon, cupro, modal, modacrylics, and triacetate); and those made from a blend of natural and synthetic fibers.

In connection with more awareness and concern with environmental issues and with a growing nostalgia for the past, 100 percent natural fibers have experienced a burgeoning popularity over the past decade. Cotton, especially, has become the fiber of choice in both the fashion apparel industry and the upholstery industry. A vegetable fiber from the cotton plant, cotton is durable and strong, and it can be adapted to create a wide variety of fabric types, such as voiles, chintzes, cotton satins, and corduroys. Cotton is easily dyed, relatively colorfast, and receptive to finishes that makes the fabric resistant to shrinkage, stains, and wrinkles.

Silk is a natural animal fiber that is extracted from the cocoons of silkworm larvae. Unlike cotton, it is a

high-maintenance natural fiber. Although silk fabrics are strong and resilient and not prone to wrinkling, they stain easily, do not withstand heat well, and most of the dyes used on silk are not very colorfast. However, in terms of elegance, luster, and vivid colors, silk is without peer.

Linen, a dressier cousin to cotton, is made from the vegetable fiber of the flax plant. Like cotton, it is strong and durable, but it is much more prone to wrinkling and creasing, and can mildew in damp conditions. One

Cotton and linen are both strong, durable fibers. These Schumacher fabrics, made of a cotton-linen blend, demonstrate how the two fibers can be fashioned into a variety of looks.

Worsted wool fabric is an ideal choice for cooler climates because of its insulating properties.

of linen's most appealing characteristics is its texture. It can be extremely nubby, drawing the eye through texture without the need for a printed pattern. Used in a blend with other materials or given a crease-resistant finish, some of linen's wrinkling proclivity can be reduced. Linen typically is more expensive than the other natural plant fiber, cotton.

Wool is another all-natural fiber used in upholstery. Made from the coats of sheep or goats, wool is valued for its insulating warmth. As a choice for chilly rooms, it is unsurpassed in comfort. Because of its warmer look and feel, wool is also a pleasing complement to the "lodge look" that has become popular in interior design. It is naturally absorbent and can retain body heat—a plus for cooler spaces in winter. Its natural absorbency, however, makes it extremely prone to stains unless it is treated with a stain-resistant substance. Wool is also subject to shrinkage and to attack by moths. Both of these problems, however, can be averted through proper treatment, making wool a durable and versatile upholstery fabric.

Almost in conjunction with the rise in popularity of natural fibers has been a strong backlash against synthetic fibers. The widespread opinion is that they look unnatural and feel stiff. When used in blends, however, synthetic fibers are extremely valuable in upholstery. The following is a guide to the most common synthetics used in upholstery blends. (More information on these and other fibers can be found in the Glossary.)

Polyester, perhaps more than any other synthetic fiber, has borne the brunt of the backlash against synthetics. However, used in the proper way, this petroleum-derived fabric can be an extremely versatile upholstery fabric. In a blend with natural fibers, it can take a low profile, allowing the natural fiber to dominate the textile's appearance. In blends, polyester makes natural fibers more utilitarian, longer-lasting, and lower in maintenance. Polyster does not stretch (which can be a problem in certain upholstery treatments), is fast-drying, and has a low absorbency—features important to a textile that's apt to undergo heavy use in the home as an upholstery fabric. It is also very strong, making blended fabrics less likely to be punctured or to tear.

Nylon is a petroleum-derived cousin of polyester that is also used primarily in blends for its inherent strength and resistance to wrinkling. However, nylon is less stain-resistant and more heat-sensitive than polyester, which means it tends to fade or discolor when exposed to prolonged sunlight. When using a blended fabric consisting of a sizeable percentage of nylon, take care to situate the upholstered furnishing out of direct sunlight. Some of the lighter-weight nylons are unsuitable as upholstery fabrics. However, because of its stretching ability, nylon is an easy material to use for conforming to the compound curves of certain complex chair shapes.

Related to polyester and nylon, acrylic fibers are also derived from petroleum. Acrylics are used in blended fabrics due to their texture—they have the soft feel, durability, and warmth of wool—plus the fact that they are stretch-resistant. Unlike wool, acrylics also have the advantage of being mothproof, and they can be lightly sponged to remove light stains. On the down side, acrylics are heat-sensitive.

Acetate is a cellulose fiber that features wood pulp as its major raw ingredient. It is more commonly used for window treatment fabrics than upholstery coverings, because of its good draping characteristics. However, it is frequently used in blends to make satins and brocades, which appear on more formal upholstered furnishings. Negative features of acetate that prevent its use by itself, without some other fiber, include heat sensitivity, absorbency, a tendency to shrink and lose shape when wet, and low durability.

Resistant to wrinkling, ripping, and puncture, synthetic fabrics have an important place in upholstery today. This fabric with a subtle swirling pattern is 100 percent Cordura nylon.

JUST BECAUSE AN UPHOLSTERY fabric doesn't consist of 100 percent natural fibers does not necessarily mean it's bad or in any way an inferior product. Many blends of synthetic or man-made fibers with natural fibers result in a more utilitarian textile that still bears the look of the natural fiber.

The blending process occurs before spinning; the various fibers are blended together, then spun to form yarns of a new variety. These blended fibers are then woven to create a fabric with a different appearance, performance, and surface quality than those of any of the individual fibers alone.

Many people prefer a blend of natural and synthetic fibers in which the natural fiber dominates the fabric's appearance while the synthetic fiber lends its utilitarian properties. The fabrics featured here are (clockwise from left) cotton-rayon and cotton-polyester; wool-nylon; linen-cotton-polyester.

A polyester-cotton mix becomes lighter, stronger, and more crease- or wrinkle-resistant than a fabric consisting of cotton by itself. But unlike an all-polyester material, the blended fabric retains the softness—the "hand"—of natural cotton.

In the early days of technology, synthetic or man-made fibers tended to look the part—they seemed in some way artificial. But continual advances in the industry mean that the product is constantly being improved. Today, synthetics can emulate any number of natural fibers, both in appearance and performance. Modified rayon, or Modal, as it is often known, looks and behaves similarly to cotton, for example.

Viscose rayon is a regenerated vegetable fiber that is chemically made, involving the processing of wood pulp. On their own, viscose rayons are not a likely upholstery choice: they are not durable, shrink-resistant, fray-free, mothproof, or static-free. To overcome these handicaps, various appropriate treatments of the fabric are necessary. When blended with cotton or linen yarns, viscose rayon fabrics have satisfactory wear. Viscose rayons are also among the least expensive of fibers, making them a common choice in blends. They are also easy to work with. In addition, the fiber is especially suited for simulating silk. Though used often in upholstery fabric blends, viscose rayon's most important use isn't as an upholstery fabric, but as a draping material.

COVERING

Once an understanding of fabric fiber content has been gleaned, it's time to consider the weave of fabric desired for an upholstered furnishing. The most common—and affordable—fabrics used to cover home furnishings are plain weaves. The pattern (if there is one) is printed directly onto the finished, woven surface of this fabric. But plain weaves are by no means the only type of fabric available. For a richer look, fabrics are woven to cre-

Left: A variety of natural and synthetic blends and 100 percent natural fabrics offers a wide range of looks. Right: Patterns can be printed on fabric, woven in, or created by using a combination of both techniques

Above: Self-colored patterns and designs create textural interest on a fabric. These fabrics are 100 percent nylon.

designs and pattern weaves involving more than one color.

To understand cost differences between fabric types, it helps to have a knowledge of the weaving process involved. Two terms that will come in handy in understanding weaves are *warp*—which refers to the threads that run parallel along the length of the material—and *weft*—those threads running across the cloth. For a more detailed look at the different types of fabric weaves and traditional woven fabrics used in upholstery, see the Glossary.

ate textural interest on the surface by means of self-colored patterns and

Right: These refreshing fabrics are known as chintz. A hallmark of the English country look, chintz is a printed cotton fabric that has been glazed.

Chapter

3

DETERMINING THE DIFFERENCE

N OT ALL UPHOLSTERED furniture is created equal. With more and more upholstery methods and materials available, the uneducated consumer would do best to follow the old adage "Buyer beware."

However, with some basic understanding of upholstery techniques and materials (see Chapter Two), risks can be reduced to a minimum. And with a working knowledge of upholstery vocabulary and very basic concepts, non-expert consumers can better process—and heed—advice from the experts themselves.

In this chapter, we've gone directly to the professionals—to the individual furniture upholsterers and to the furniture manufacturers themselves—for a list of consumer tips on how to distinguish quality upholstery work from shoddy craftsmanship. With this primer in hand, any consumer should be able to walk away with a newly upholstered furnishing that will bring years of gratification and few, if any, regrets.

• *Before entering the first furniture store or upholstery shop, identify where you want the upholstered furnishing to be situated in the home and how you expect it to be used.*

Whether a sofa or chair is to be situated in a frequently used, casual family room or in a more formal and less often used living room or parlor determines a lot about the style and materials needed for the upholstery treatment. Also, be realistic about other concerns that will have an impact on whether or not a particular type of upholstered piece will work for you—factors such as the presence of children and pets in the household. All must be figured into the picture before an informed upholstery decision can be made.

Above: The light colors selected for this sofa are right for the cheerful mood of the room, but they might not be a good choice if this is the family dog's favorite spot.

Opposite: This beautiful settee with its delicately tufted seat back is at home among elegant Corinthian columns.

• *In buying manufactured uphol-*
stered furniture, consider the
brand name.

"In buying upholstered furniture, it's especially important to find a recognizable brand name you can trust," says Don Essenberg, merchandise manager for the upholstery division at Broyhill Furniture Industries, Inc.

"With upholstered furniture, it's not that difficult to set up manufacturing. This means a lot of companies that are in business today won't be tomorrow. For the consumer, selecting a brand-name manufacturer is further insurance of quality," says Essenberg. "It's important to the consumer to know that if something goes wrong with the furnishing, the manufacturer will still be in business to correct the problem."

Reputable manufacturers typically will be honest with potential buyers, labeling any fabric warnings and identifying construction methods. Even here, though, some care needs to be exercised by the consumer. Some mid-price-point manufacturers (such as Broyhill) may identify sofa construction as eight-way, hand-tied coils. This is literally correct, but the coils are pre-tied, then they are dropped into the unit by a manufacturing process. This differs from an individually hand-crafted sofa where the coils are, in fact, tied by hand directly onto the furnishing (a process still used by upper-end manufacturers such as Baker). In terms of quality, the pre-tied piece features less craftsmanship and the lower quality that that entails. In addition, brand-name manufacturers will identify whether or not an upholstered piece utilizes hardwood for the furniture frame. Lesser-known or smaller manufacturers may or may not, leaving the consumer with the risk of purchasing an upholstered furnishing that may not be sturdy enough to withstand years of wear.

When shopping for uphol-
stered furniture, consider the
brand name. Reputable manu-
facturers should label fabrics
and identify construction
methods that are invisible
to the eye.

sible for any but the most savvy of consumers to recognize as affecting quality. This is where it's important to work with a reputable retailer.

Find someone who's been in the business for years, who has a reputation for honesty, and who stands behind the merchandise that he or she sells. A quality retailer is knowledgeable about the merchandise and is receptive to any questions you might have. It is extremely important to ask questions in order to ensure that you get the best possible piece for your needs. If the particular salesperson working the floor at the time you are shopping is unable to provide satisfactory answers, ask to speak with a supervisor. Explain that it's important for you to understand fully what your options are before making a selection. No one should have hurt feelings. It's unreasonable to think that a salesperson two days into the job will have the expertise necessary to provide you with comprehensive answers to your questions. But there's no excuse for a supervisor or manager being inadequately informed. If you've found a furnishing you like, but you can't get enough detailed information on its construction, keep climbing the ladder. Eventually, someone should be able to answer all your questions about the piece—and should respect your tenacity in wanting the facts essential for a smart buy.

Once you've found a furnishing you like, don't be afraid to ask questions. A reputable retailer should be happy to address your concerns.

• *In addition to buying a brand name, make your selection from a reputable retailer.*

As illustrated by the subtle difference between pre-tied and custom-tied coil springs, both of which bear the identification "eight-way hand-tied coil springs," upholstered furnishings entail some technical construction methods that may be all but impos-

• *Don't be misled by price. It's one yardstick, but not an absolute measurement of quality.*

Both the individual upholstery shop owner and the upholstered furniture manufacturer are clear on this point: price tags can deceive.

"Price isn't always a reliable indicator of quality," insists master upholsterer David Draper of David Draper Designs, Inc., a Des Moines, Iowa, custom upholstery shop that caters to the interior design industry. Just because a sofa or upholstered chair seems comparatively expensive is no

guarantee that it features the highest standards in materials or methods of construction. Your retailer may be passing on high overhead expenses, or you may be paying more for a new design from a manufacturer that has more to do with "look" than with actual quality.

With today's upholstered furniture, there is an unfortunate trend in "over-covering" the frame—putting expensive, high-end fabric over an inferior furnishing. The consumer is often asked to pay the higher price for a high-quality furnishing only to

Sometimes it's necessary to reach underneath a piece of upholstered furniture to test for quality. Tension on the underside indicates coil springs and webbing— both signs of quality manufacturing.

These dining chairs have a slightly ethereal quality. On the inside, they should still feature the materials and methods of construction that will ensure their longevity.

furniture doesn't have tension, it isn't top of the line," warns Draper. "This will indicate a no-sag spring construction or some other type of construction other than coil springs and webbing beneath the dustcover"—methods and materials you'll want to avoid if seeking a high-quality piece.

• Highest-quality upholstered furnishings feature eight-way hand-tied coil-spring construction.

This construction method refers to the type of springs (coil), as well as to how they are held in place (the construction method). Both the materials and the method affect quality. An eight-way hand-tie means that the coil springs are held in place across the top by eight hand-tied knots of a row of cord made of material such as Italian jute or imported hemp. This tying method ensures that the springs lie smooth across the furnishing. The high number of knots also means that if one rope of webbing should break, there are still six knots holding the piece in place—enough so that you probably won't ever know that there has been breakage, unless you are having the piece reupholstered for decorative reasons. (Four-way knots may be adequate, but they won't provide the furniture with the longevity that is offered by eight-way knots.)

obtain the designer fabric, without gaining the benefits of a quality-constructed piece of furniture.

• When unsure about quality, do the touch test. Feel beneath the furniture's skirt to determine the difference.

"The best rule of thumb to ensure quality for the untrained eye is a quick test—reaching underneath the skirt to the bottom of a sofa or chair," says Draper. If you feel tension at the bottom (underside) of the upholstered piece, this indicates coil springs and webbing—the hallmark of quality that you are seeking. "If the

"When the coil springs are hand-tied smoothly and evenly, with burlap

Left: Eight-way hand-tied coil
springs indicate a high-
quality upholstered furnishing, in which you shouldn't
feel the springs through
the cushions.

over the padding, you shouldn't be able to feel the springs at all," says Draper. "There's no tipping at the crown. On a cheap hand-tie, on the other hand, you can feel the edges of the coil springs underneath the cushion."

Mid-price-point furnishings that use a drop-in suspension method for eight-way hand-tied coil spring units are distinctly different from the high-end furnishings that feature the entirely hand-crafted, custom process that more accurately deserves the name of eight-way hand-tied coil springs. There are two major differences between the pre-tied drop-in and custom-tied pieces. Both feature coil springs, but those that have been pre-tied are built and assembled in advance to fit a standard chair or sofa size. This entails less manual labor and less customization or old-style craftsmanship than when the springs are individually tied onto the furnishing. In addition, the pre-tied, drop-in coil units are typically tied with Number 9 wire, not webbing. "Wire

Below: Mid-priced furnishings often feature eight-way hand-tied coil springs that have been suspended as one unit rather than placed individually.

will break, whereas webbing will not," says Draper. "Drop-in coil spring units aren't bad for the price, but they don't feature the quality of the real eight-way hand-tie."

The best materials on an eight-way hand-tied coil spring are a ten-pound (16kg) LMC (seat spring) with 3½-to-4-inch (8.8 to 10cm) jute webbing and a nine-pound (4.1kg) back spring. "In addition, Number 14 barb tacks should be used with the webbing," says Draper. Properly executed eight-way hand-tied coil springs also have the webbing material doubled at the stress points, to eliminate stretch.

Lower-quality no-sag springs, in contrast, are designed to give. "This is what results in a warped front deck rail [underneath the cushion, between the two front legs of a chair]," explains Draper.

Unlike hand-tied coil springs, no-sag or zigzag springs are stretched and nailed to the back and front rails of the furnishing. "This isn't bad furniture, but it is a less expensive construction method that's necessary to bring the price down for some medium- to lower-priced furnishings, which the market demands," says Draper.

On the cheapest upholstered furniture, springs may constitute an equalizer unit—tension springs coated in plastic, which look something like old fencing wire. "This furniture isn't good after six months," warns Draper. "You can't tear a new furnishing's deck apart to see if it's constructed with no-sag springs or an equalizer unit, but you can sure tell the difference between these and coil springs by the touch."

DETERMINING THE DIFFERENCE

• *Upholstered furniture is only as good as its frame. Hardwood is still the best material for longevity.*

Consumers should not be shy in insisting on knowing what kind of wood is beneath the upholstery. An all-hardwood frame remains the best indicator of quality, providing years of enjoyment without splitting, warping, or breaking. Knowing that the piece is hardwood is imperative, since many lower-end manufacturers make a common practice of framing with plywood or particle board. Beneath the attractive upholstery fabric, the frame is concealed. The buyer will never know what's there without asking. Oak is upholsterers' preferred framing material, but poplar and cottonwood are also acceptable.

• *Make sure no corners have been cut on the amount of framing material.*

To withstand weight and years of wear and tear, a furnishing's wood framing rails should be a full inch (2.5cm) or even 1¼ inches (3.1cm) in width. Some lower-end manufacturers may attempt to cut corners by using less, but not without endangering the consumer. This is one area in which the manufacturer can't afford to skimp without sacrificing safety. A brand-name and a reliable retailer are the best starting points to ensure against

this, but asking questions regarding the width of the rails is still a good idea to be completely sure.

• *Kiln-dried hardwood is preferable to air-dried wood.*

It may sound picky, but even the method by which the wood framing material is dried affects the quality and longevity of the upholstered furnishing. Most industry experts agree that a kiln-dried hardwood is more durable and long-lasting than wood that has been dried in the open air. Most major furniture manufacturers make this information readily available to the consumer.

A frame made of a hardwood such as oak is the best indicator of quality. Don't be afraid to ask what's inside an upholstered furnishing.

• *Look for dowel construction in the wood frame as a signpost of quality.*

Dowel joinery refers to the method in which the wooden parts of a furniture frame are held together, or joined, by use of a dowel—a pin or peg of wood that slips in between two corresponding pieces of furniture frame through holes in each one, to hold the frame members in place. Because it is actually fitted together, the frame constructed with dowels will hold longer and more securely than the frame joined with air staples and glue. Double dowel-pin construction is recommended for its solid, holding

powers—traits just as important on upholstered furnishings as on exposed wood pieces.

• *Investigate exposed wood areas closely. Finely finished pieces are indicative of overall quality of materials and methods.*

Although many upholstered furnishings are all-upholstered, with no exposed wood parts, others have legs, feet, or a portion of arms exposed in natural wood. The quality of the finish on these exposed areas—however scant they may be—is a good indicator of the overall quality of an uphol-

Inspect the quality of exposed wood parts. This is often a good indication of the overall quality of a piece.

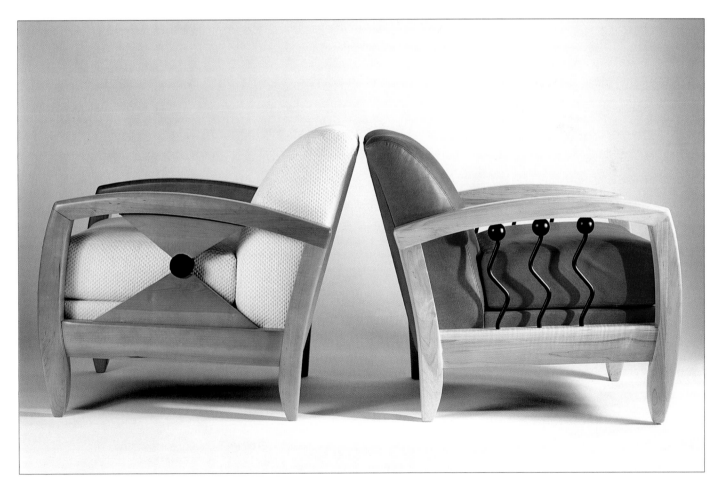

stered piece. The rule is, the finer the finish, the finer the upholstery work in general.

• *For the best cushions, buy those filled with HR (high resiliency) foam.*

HR, or high-resiliency, polyurethane foam is designed to keep its shape with heavy use and over a long period of time. Among manufacturers and individual upholsterers alike, it has the best reputation for quality of any of the foams or filling materials for upholstered seating cushions. The professionals appreciate the foam's longevity and its recovery powers (how it regains its shape after use). They also like the way the foam holds its lines without causing the fabric covering to wrinkle. However, even with a quality material such as HR foam, some additional precautions should be taken regarding the amount of foam used in the cushions and the compression factor (which varies according to the manufacturer's or upholsterer's specifications) of the foam itself.

Upholsterers have been able to reach a consensus that HR 30—with a compression factor of thirty—is ideal for seat cushions. The compression factor refers to the amount of air that is present in the foam. The higher the compression number, the less air is in the foam and the harder

the foam will feel. A compression factor of thirty is recommended for general use. When the only person to be sitting on a sofa or chair is extremely small (weighing less than one hundred pounds [45.4kg]), a lower compression factor is recommended, as HR 30 will produce a seat that is too hard and uncomfortable for such a lightweight person. Because of the overall resilience of HR foam, it may be specified at a compression factor lower than thirty among some mid-price-point manufacturers without any real sacrifice in durability and, perhaps, with a slight gain in softness and comfort.

Above: Long after the owner tires of this zebra-print fabric, the HR polyurethane foam cushions will retain their original shape.

Opposite: For sofa cushions like these, it's important to balance durability with softness. HR foam between two and four inches (5 to 10cm) thick and with a compression factor of 30 is ideal for many people's needs.

A thickness of between two and four inches (5 to 10cm) is recommended for HR foam cushions. A cushion thicker than four inches (10cm) with a compression factor of thirty will produce an uncomfortable seat. A density of less than 1.8 inches (4.5cm) will result, even with HR foam, in a pancake effect in which the foam will compress and not regain its former shape.

"With so many options in cushion fillings, from solid foam to solid foam in Dacron to down fillings, to solid-foam cushions with coil springs, the consumer should ask a lot of questions," says Essenberg.

One of the newest cushion options is called coil-on-coil seating, in which solid foam cushions are used with springs, then placed on top of a coil suspension system. Furniture manufacturers face higher costs for using coil-on-coil seating in place of HR foam over hand-tied coil springs. This expense, of course, is passed along to the consumer. According to Essenberg, his company (Broyhill) is still waiting to determine whether or not there is an actual comfort and longevity advantage to this newer type of seating system before making the change from HR foam.

• *Old-fashioned pure foam rubber is still available as a cushion material, but even this quality substance—the best in times past—is surpassed by the newer HR foam.*

Especially with contemporary classics—sculptural furnishings designed by architects or important designers and put into production by renowned

Today, HR foam is considered superior to the pure foam rubber that was used in contemporary classics such as the Barcelona chair designed by Mies van der Rohe.

polyurethane foam represents an improvement over pure foam rubber and is thus the new paradigm of quality in the manufactured furniture industry.

Although pin-core foam rubber is still available (for approximately $125 a sheet and from a very limited number of distributors), it is no longer regarded as the ultimate quality material. It has a tendency to dry and crack, eventually turning into a grainy, flourlike substance. Sometimes, when hitting a foam rubber–filled cushion to clean it, a yellowish powder will leak from the cushion seams. This is not dust, but deteriorated foam rubber. In contrast, HR polyurethane foam won't break down into powder. As one industry professional describes it, "Foam rubber has gone the way of plaster walls in home interiors. Plaster has been all but replaced by Sheetrock, and foam rubber has been replaced by HR foam."

• *Down-filled cushions are unsurpassed in comfort, but they bear two price tags worth noting up front—a higher dollar cost and higher maintenance.*

Even the most vocal advocates of HR foam as the cushion filling of choice and quality agree that, when it comes to sink-down, sybaritic comfort, nothing exceeds soft, squishy goose down as a cushion filling. Down welcomes the body immediately, con-

Old-fashioned goose down will always have a place as a filling. Down cushions are more expensive and require more maintenance than foam, but they can't be beat for sink-down comfort.

manufacturers such as Knoll between the 1940s and the 1960s—foam rubber was the cushion filling of choice. It represented the highest available quality at the time and, in turn, bore a lofty price tag. But over time, pure latex foam rubber shows signs of deterioration, resulting in the need for a more durable cushion material. HR

forming to its shape. While the initial feel is instant comfort, for the fussy homeowner who cares about visual details, down cushions can be a headache. They require fluffing after each sitting in order to retain that soft, feel-good sensation and to regain their puffy, full shape. Also, down is much more expensive than other types of filling—even the highest-quality varieties of foam. And for the fuller-figured sitter, down is not flattering. It leaves a tell-tale imprint of body size that no baggy clothing can disguise.

• *To determine seating comfort, use your eye—then your body—as a guide.*

Suppose you're in a situation where a retailer can't be relied upon to provide manufacturer information such as a tag sale, a garage sale, or a flea market. In those instances, you have to wing it and make a decision whether or not to purchase an upholstered seating piece by using only your own judgment. But even here, you have more information at your disposal than you might imagine. The relative comfort of an upholstered furnishing should be an indicator of quality. Let common sense be your guide.

First, evaluate the piece with your eye. If its generous proportions and thick, deep cushions suggest blissful comfort, follow up with the seat test.

Plop down on the piece in whatever position you're likely to take when you are relaxing at home. Does the feel of the furnishing match the look of comfort suggested by its lines? If not, then something is probably not what it should be in the upholstery job. Inferior materials, poor construction methods, or both, are most likely to blame. If a furnishing that should feel luxuriant based on its appearance is far too firm, chances are good that it is an inexpensive grade of furniture. On the other hand, a tight-seat

If you intend to spend time sitting in a chair, it needs to be comfortable. Subject every chair to the seat test before making a purchase.

upholstered piece that looks firm to the eye should be just that to the body; anything less, and there is probably a problem with quality.

• Look at the fabric application: is it even and centered?

In one sense, it's easy to distinguish between better qualities of upholstered furnishings and those of inferior workmanship just by looking at the fabric application. On the good pieces, floral patterns are precisely centered, with the mass of the print in the middle of the furniture and the smaller print repeats falling off to the sides. Stripes are particularly good yardsticks for determining quality upholstery work: it's easy to get the repeats out of line for a disjointed look. On better upholstered furnishings, the stripe patterns will match from the back cushion to the seat cushion, from the rolled sofa arm to the bottom of the sofa side.

• Judge the upholstery work by the visual evidence of tailoring, paying special attention to the sofa or chair skirt.

Skirts on sofas and chairs say a lot about the character and quality of the overall upholstered piece. On better furnishings, skirts have a tailored look that is apparent even to the most untrained eye. The skirt will be even across the entire length of the furnishing, it will look neat, and it will retain its shape without falling limply to one side or another.

• Self-lined skirts are superior to those made with stiff rubberized cloth.

A self-lined skirt refers to a chair or sofa skirt that has been backed with an additional lining of denim or muslin for greater strength and tailoring, and that has also been treated with a Pelon stiffener. Self-lined skirts require more time to produce, and thus are more expensive, but they hold their shape far better and longer

Quality upholstered furniture can sometimes be judged by its fabric. Note how the floral fabric on this sofa is properly centered; also, the pattern matches from back cushion to seat cushion.

than those without lining. Many upholsterers today cut corners on skirts by using a stiff rubberized cloth, which eliminates the need for putting in Pelon. According to the true upholstery craftspersons, this is just a way of skimping to save money at the expense of quality.

• *Better upholstery craftsmanship features padding/filling between frame and fabric—not fabric nailed to a bare frame.*

Fewer companies follow the old-fashioned approach of applying filler and padding in between the chair or sofa frame rails and the upholstery fabric, but that doesn't change the need for such a quality measure. Fabric that is pulled taut and tacked to a bare frame is an accident waiting to happen—and is especially susceptible to tearing and ripping from the bumps or accidental blows often delivered by young children. An old-style upholsterer, when re-covering any chair or sofa, will take the time and expense to apply a layer of burlap (or a good, strong synthetic fabric) to fill in between the frame rails. The upholsterer will then top the burlap with a layer of cotton batting, bonded Dacron, or some other kind of padding before covering with the outer fabric. It is important that the fabric is not nailed to a bare frame but has some protective bulk beneath it. When you can push on an outer arm and feel the fabric give, you know the upholstery work is not top-grade craftsmanship.

• *Quality pieces feature cushions on which the boxing is consistent.*

An easy test of quality that doesn't require seeking answers to questions

Opposite: This lighthearted love seat was carefully crafted. Just look at the boxing, the band between the top and bottom of the cushion, to tell. It should be the same height all along the cushion.

Below: An old-style upholsterer will apply burlap to a frame, then add a layer of cotton batting or other padding before covering the chair with the outer fabric.

from an outside source involves looking at a chair or sofa's cushions for uniformity. Make sure the boxing, the band between the top and bottom of a cushion, is the same height all along the cushion width. This is a sign of careful craftsmanship and quality. If it is inconsistent and wavy, inferior stuffing materials within the cushions may be the culprit, along with a shoddy approach to craftsmanship and manufacturing.

• *Look for upholstery fabric applications that look laid on, not pulled on.*

A pet peeve of many upholsterers is fabric that has been pulled too tightly, as if to squeeze out every last square inch of usable goods. This tight treatment will catch at the seams, and is not as desirable as one in which the fabric lays smoothly and evenly, as though it has fallen naturally into place without having had the life pulled out of it.

• *Be prepared to make an upholstery selection knowing that fabric is the single most confusing element of the furnishing.*

Every upholsterer and upholstered furniture manufacturer is in agreement: there is absolutely no way to determine a fabric's durability based on its appearance or its price. What looks good to the eye and feels good

to the hand may be completely wrong as an upholstery fabric for your furnishing's intended use. This differs from the past, when materials could be judged accurately for durability by their weight. With the huge influx of synthetics on the market, a fabric's "hand" and weight are no longer reliable determiners of its quality. Nylon and newer synthetics may lighten a fabric's weight, but improve its overall quality by making it wrinkle-free and able to hold its shape longer.

An upholstered furnishing should never look as if it's about to burst. The fabric on this easy chair is smooth without being too taut.

• *To determine a fabric's quality, you must know its fiber content.*

Knowing precisely what a fabric is comprised of is the only safe way of predicting how long or well the fabric will wear as an upholstery covering.

• *The more heavily woven fabrics are more durable in general, but even with these weaves, be sure the fabric is fully woven and not outfitted with a rubberized backing.*

The only reason for a rubberized backing on an upholstery fabric is to conceal the fact that there is a low thread count per square inch. Although the fabric may, in fact, be 100 percent nylon, if the thread count has been reduced enough to necessitate a rubberized backing, the fabric really isn't a full fabric. Instead, it's more like screen, with open, porous places that require filling with a backing. It naturally follows that, in fabrics with a lower thread count and rubberized backings, quality and durability suffer. Look on the armcap of a sofa or chair for information on whether the upholstery is fully woven or is woven with a rubberized backing, or ask your salesperson.

Heavy woven fabrics are usually the most durable. However, the surest way to determine the strength of a fabric is to find out its fiber content.

- *As with bedding, look for a high thread count on better upholstery fabrics.*

Just as better bedding directly correlates to an increased thread count per square inch, so does upholstery fabric rely on a close weave for quality.

- *Check the mill's abrasion rating of a fabric before determining whether or not it's appropriate for the use you intend.*

Fabrics are given abrasion ratings as consumer guides to how the fabric may best be put to use. The ratings are: delicate durability duty, light duty, medium duty, and heavy durability duty. It is a myth that the most expensive fabrics are the most durable. If you are concerned about how a fabric

will wear, ask the retailer. Some manufacturers print cautions on their furniture, and may advise consumers against covering any reclining furnishing with delicate or light duty fabrics. Much of the fear in fabric selection can be alleviated by selecting a reputable, knowledgeable retailer.

- *For an antique restoration, there is no substitute for the old-style upholstery approach.*

When having an antique reupholstered, the process is much the same as it was a century ago, with the exception of sofas now featuring coil-spring construction and eight-way hand-ties. Above the coil-spring construction and webbing, just as it was in yesteryear, a ten-ounce (0.3kg) woven burlap should be applied, fol-

A distinctive chair in need of restoration. For an antique, it's best to seek out an upholsterer familiar with traditional methods.

The same chair shown on the
previous page after it has
been reupholstered.
Traditional techniques such
as using hog's hair as filling
are often preferable when
reupholstering an antique.

lowed by jute edge rolls along the edges, filled with crushed paper fibers and wadding wrapped with jute for a good hard edge. On top of this finger roll (which prevents the sitter from feeling any of the frame) is placed curled hog's hair (actually a combination of 85 percent hog's hair and 15 percent horsehair) as the stuffing for a tight-seat upholstered piece. (Spanish moss is preferable to hog's hair, but is no longer readily available. And sisal is no longer rec-ommended, as it tends to mildew and create an unpleasant odor.) Over the hog's hair, cotton batting is placed, topped with muslin (actually a deck-ing denim in a beige or off-white, since today's muslin is low quality and likely to tear easily, like cheese-cloth) as a pre-covering to smooth out the padding. Over the pre-cover-ing, the surface fabric is aligned and centered with the proper cuts and pleats, for a fully restored uphol-stered furnishing.

Chapter

4

A MATTER OF STYLE

During my stint as design editor of a national decorating magazine, I had the opportunity, one day each year, to do nothing but field calls from readers to a toll-free phone number set up just to help them with the number one decorating problem: getting started with choosing a style. It was my job on the phone line to assist callers with decorating issues—any problems they might be having, from how to incorporate a large-screen television into a family room without creating an eyesore to how to choose an appropriate new lamp for a small antique table. Some of the callers did have specific, nuts-and-bolts design problems with which they needed help. The vast majority of others, though, had a much bigger issue to address first—how to determine their personal style.

After manning the phone line and visiting with readers across the country when I traveled to present decorating seminars, I finally realized just how pervasive, and deeply troubling,

Our homes reflect who we are. Finding your own personal style requires an understanding of your preferences and a willingness to experiment.

the problem of identifying just the right "look" for our homes can be. People intuitively want to reflect their personalities in their home decor, but when it's time to begin, many become paralyzed with insecurity. So afraid are they of making a decorating gaffe that would be laughable to a more trained eye, or to the eye of a sophisticated friend, that they can't seem to galvanize their personal tastes into design solutions that reflect who they really are.

For example, one caller was lamenting the difficulty of choosing a color to paint her basement rec room. We talked about favorite colors, hues that made her feel good, and the colors in her wardrobe closet, until I was pretty sure she was equipped to make

her own decision. Then, she stopped me in my tracks with one question: "Well, what do *you* think my favorite color should be?"

Clearly some of us have a longer way to go than others when it comes to evaluating our aesthetic and lifestyle preferences—and being secure enough to translate those tastes into design elements that reflect our personalities in the home.

Short of visiting a therapist about ego issues, though, the process really doesn't have to be painful. Instead, it can be fun, like taking one of those magazine quizzes that are designed to put us in touch with our feelings. This is no major analysis, just a quick probing tool to find out what we really want.

The owner of this home likes to read, and has created a comfortable area with an overstuffed chair and proper lighting to indulge this hobby.

Consider how upholstered
furnishings will complement
other pieces you own, and
look beyond just fabric. The
graceful curve of this covered
bench silently echoes the
curled base of the table.

UPHOLSTERY
AS AN INTEGRAL PART
of a Larger Plan

UPHOLSTERED FURNITURE ISN'T an island unto itself. It's an integral part of a larger design scheme, which is the entire room. To make an appropriate decision on what kind of upholstered piece to purchase or have covered, it's paramount first to know clearly what one's personal style is all about, to identify the core game plan for the broader space, and to then ensure that the upholstered furnishings fit seamlessly into that overall scheme.

The starting point isn't in the middle of a home furnishings gallery, where picking and choosing is the task at hand; it's in the mind, where only you are capable of creating an unambiguous statement about who you are.

One reason that attempting to imbue your home with your personal style can be so intimidating to non-professionals is that most people do not have a clearly defined sense of a style that they want to adhere to. Most people's tastes are full of variables and ambiguities that do not match up cleanly with any one preconceived "look." Personal style, by definition, isn't one look, one school of design that you can diagram and appropriate for yourself. What constitutes personal style for your best friend may be totally different from what proves to be your own personal style. Unlike the more generic concept of style, *personal* style is one-of-a-kind. It's an individual handprint that you freely impress on your home environment, in much the same way that you choose your own tastes in clothing. Accept that your style will be a mix of design styles.

Your personal style is something that you alone are qualified to define. Don't be afraid to combine elements of different styles. In this room, classical prints are paired with a zebra rug, resulting in a strong statement of style.

The big, bold scarves you admire as your friend's trademark may look nothing short of ridiculous draped around your own neck. Your personal style may be more casual, less studied, than that. Your badge may be ethnic jewelry—funky necklaces you've found on travels or managed to turn up on routine shopping expeditions. Whether designer scarves or folk art jewelry, each of these elements is a statement of personal style. Each one is equally valid, equally correct. The only possible mistake would be attempting to claim as your own trademark a look that doesn't feel right for you, one that doesn't capture your fancy and tell the world who you honestly believe you are or want to be.

The only difference between personal style in your wardrobe and in your home decor is who is wearing the expressions of individual taste—you or your home. Upholstered furnishings should be every bit as indicative of who you are as the suit on your back or the shoes on your feet.

And just because upholstered pieces may, for you, represent comfort above all else, this doesn't mean they are exempt from fitting into the larger scheme of the room's personality. Big, clunky recliners that made no particular style statement may have sufficed in your parents' den, but we've evolved a long way aesthetically since then. Consider upholstered pieces as among your most important design elements, invaluable decorating tools at your disposal to grace your living environment with one-of-a-kind verve and a well-defined mood.

Upholstered furnishings will usually play an important role in the design of a room. The bold striped chairs that flank the sofa in this room are a prime example.

Whether or not you plan to hire an interior designer, it's helpful to reflect on your own preferences. Do you like gilded objects such as this chair?

DESIGNER'S CHECK LIST:
Learning Who You Are, What You Want

M OST INTERIOR DESIGNERS I know tend to employ the same process for communicating with their clients who have trouble articulating the looks that they want: they ask questions. And more questions. Then they have their clients scour decorating magazines, pulling pages with photographs of rooms they find appealing and wouldn't mind having as spaces in their own homes. You don't need a high-dollar designer to guide you through the process, however. You can do it yourself. Get started by taking time to answer the following questions honestly.

- Do I consider myself a trend-setter and trailblazer, a traditionalist, or something in between?

- Am I quiet and conservative, or do I like to make waves?

• Do I admire understated elegance, or do I gravitate toward bolder statements of finery?

• If forced to pick one, would I choose Victorians' highly decorative furniture or Shaker's bare-bones simplicity?

• Do I seek out serene places and people, or those that stimulate the senses with a constant adrenaline flow?

• Do I think of myself as up-front and straight-shooting or as more mysterious, always holding something back?

• Which kind of companions do I seek out as most interesting, comfortable, pleasant, and fun to be with?

• Do I prefer spending my free time in the company of others or by myself?

This basement rec room is not for the faint of heart. Patterns and colors collide everywhere, from the bright red enameled walls to the table and multihued vinyl-covered chairs.

The use of black can be very dramatic. A high-gloss black chair rail serves as a frame for the classically inspired wallpaper below. The black and gilt chair is a perfect complement, and its upholstery brings out the warmer tones in the wallpaper.

• Do I feel excited about the future, embracing technology and ever-changing trends, or am I more comfortable with things the way they are, perhaps even nostalgic for the "good old days"?

• Which artist do I prefer: Monet, Matisse, or Grandma Moses?

• Which comes first for me: family or career?

• Am I a romantic?

• Which New York museum building do I like better—the modern Guggenheim, or the classic Metropolitan?

• Am I more comfortable in jeans and T-shirt or in dressier clothes?

• Do I like coordinated ensembles in my wardrobe for a put-together look or do I enjoy a more free-wheeling mix-and-match approach to dress?

• Which two colors appear with the most frequency in my closet?

• Is my closet's apparel dominated by solids or prints?

• Are my moods consistent from day to day or are they ever-changing?

• Overall, am I exuberant, quietly optimistic, or restrained and subdued?

• Is my idea of a good time kicking back and plopping my feet on the coffee table or dressing for a large and lively dinner party?

• Am I an outdoor person or do I prefer indoor pursuits for my leisure time?

• Are pets and children a part of my life's game plan?

• If forced to choose only one, which music would I prefer: classical, jazz, rock, or country?

• Which pastime appeals to me the most: reading, watching TV or videos, or listening to music?

• Which meal would I choose: Tex-Mex beef enchiladas, pasta with pesto, duck à l'orange, or steak hot off the grill?

• How much value do I place on appearances—of both places and people?

• How important are others' opinions of me?

• Which travel destination would I choose: Paris or the countryside in the south of France?

• Do I like streamlined organization or am I more comfortable with a looser approach?

• Which sounds like more fun: attending a local flea market or a Sotheby's auction?

• Do I find an abundance of objects disquieting, needing everything concealed to think clearly

Do you like to travel? This room almost tells a story through furniture and objects collected from around the world. The upholstered furnishings help break up some of the heavier wood pieces in the room.

A formal dining room is essential for someone who likes to entertain, but formal doesn't have to mean boring. The simple striped fabric used on most of the dining chairs is interrupted by a burst of flowered upholstery at either end of the table.

and have peace of mind, or do I take delight in an exposed array of collectibles?

• For a weekend trek, would I enjoy camping outdoors, staying in a quaint B & B or historic inn, spending the night in a luxury hotel, or staying at the Day's Inn?

• How often do I have friends or business associates over to the house?

• When entertaining, am I more comfortable with a formal, sit-down dinner or a serve-yourself buffet of hors d'oeuvres?

• How much advance notice do I need to plan a weekend excursion—at least a week, a couple of days, or about a minute?

• Which dinnerware would I choose: an heirloom pattern, Scandinavian modern, or a local potter's handiwork?

• Where would my spirit find greatest solace: in a warm, enveloping den with shutters closed and a crackling fire at the hearth, or in an open, sunny space with daylight streaming in through walls of glass expanses?

- Do I prefer looking at family pictures or works by an unfamiliar artist?

- Do I value the precision of manufactured goods or the imperfections of hand-crafted objects?

- How do I perceive my connection to the natural environment: intensely close, moderate, or remote?

- On a pretty day, would I choose a picnic by the river or a cozy family dinner at a well-dressed table indoors?

- Do I like fine, sculptural forms and finishes or more rugged looks that are earthy and full of texture?

- Do my closest friends have much in common or are they a diverse, seemingly unrelated group?

- In an art gallery, am I comforted by the pared-down simplicity or put off by the chill?

- Do I like abstract or concrete, literal thought?

- When presenting a gift, do I care about the wrapping or consider only the contents?

- Am I willing to go to a little extra time and trouble to look good or is getting on with the other business of my life more urgent?

If you took the time to consider each question carefully and respond honestly, you now most likely have a better idea of who you are than you did before. Each answer not only helps you to identify your personality in more definite terms, it also helps point you toward your personal style of decorating.

If, for example, your answer to the last question was no, that you would rather get on with the business of your life than spend extra time on your appearance, it means you tend toward a decorating style that is low-maintenance, with comfort and life-style ease taking priority over fussier housekeeping chores associated with some design styles. (No down cushions for you!) Likewise, if you an-

Opposite: Not every room needs a rug. Diamond parquet floors, a classically styled upholstered chair, and puddled drapes combine to create a formal look.

Below: The wood floors in this home were intentionally left bare. The upholstered dining chairs with skirts to the floor help soften the room, preventing the appearance of too much wood.

swered the next to the last question by saying you do care about a gift's wrapping, then details mean a lot to you in home design, too. The piping, fringe trim, or perfectly pleated skirt on an upholstered chair can make all the difference in how you feel about the entire room.

Opposite: White upholstered dining chairs are elegant, but you'll want to consider the realities of your lifestyle before selecting fabrics that show dirt so easily.

Below: Don't be afraid to mix several colors in one room. Fabrics in sherbet-like pastels are combined in this sunny room for a light and airy effect.

If your answers to some of the questions indicated that you are quiet and reflective and prefer simplicity over extravagance, then a serene, monochromatic palette and contemporary or understated traditional design may be your design preference. If you are nostalgic and romantic, then a frillier space that is saturated with lace and pastels, such as cottage country style may be your ticket. If you are a traditionalist who enjoys trips to Paris, the Metropolitan, classical music, and a feast of duck à l'orange, then a classic, formal design with vintage or reproduction pieces may be more appealing to you than the more casual and transitional country or contemporary looks. If you are an outdoors person and environmentalist, most comfortable in a sunny space, then an upbeat interior of organic fabrics that emphasize light and texture over pattern and contrived colors is probably preferable to you—perhaps either in a contemporary or country motif. If you are moody and always holding back, a dramatic contemporary space that relies on plays of light and shadow, candlelight reflection onto glass, and a somber palette of black and gray with accents of red may be perfect for expressing who you really are.

Don't be concerned if some of your answers suggest inconsistency. This only means you are normal. If, overall, you seem to prefer simple understatement and possess a contemporary sensibility that's open to technology, trends, and the future, it's not "wrong" to also take delight in arrays of collectibles. Keep this apparent inconsistency in mind as only one more expression of who you are—then create room spaces that take into account *all* facets of your personality. The style of your rooms can reflect your complexity. Nobody says you can only be one way, day in and day out. The beauty of personal style is that it allows expression of all personality traits, even those that may seem aberrant to the overall picture of who you are.

GENERIC DESIGN STYLES:
Contemporary, Traditional, Transitional, Eclectic, and Country

Black leather and hardwood floors combine for a contemporary look. This room has a museum-display quality: the sculptural furnishings stand alone and invite study.

WHILE EACH HOMEOWNER'S personal style is unique, it can be very helpful to think of it as a variation on a larger generic design style. Based on your answers to the earlier questionnaire, can you deter- mine which design style your taste is most akin to? The advantage of being able to identify your preferred look as part of a particular design school is that it equips you with guidelines and enormous knowledge of how to dec-

Contemporary rooms may still include an antique or two. Sometimes selecting an unexpected fabric for an antique will update the piece interestingly.

orate within the framework of that style. But don't think there's anything rigid about being associated with one style or another: each decorating style is intended to ease the way for you in expressing yourself, not to stifle or constrain you into any predetermined mold that's not an easy, natural fit. While you may be a traditionalist at heart, a resoundingly trendsetting contemporary theme may need to declare itself in your personality—and your home. That's okay. Use each style's identifying characteristics to explore ways of expressing your innermost self, even when there's an overlap between distinct styles.

CONTEMPORARY

Some consumers have a fixed image of contemporary style: stark Danish modern; high-tech minimalist; hard-edged; unrealistically clean and pared down; monochromatic, nonexpressive, and chilly overall. Contemporary style can be any of these, but it can also be a look that incorporates none of them. To understand whether or not your personal style falls into the contemporary camp, it's important to get beyond the easy stereotypes and rigid assumptions, to view contemporary design as the all-encompassing canvas of various modern sensibilities in all their different manifestations.

Contemporary design is a decorating style that rejects the traditional forms, finishes, and motifs of the past for new ones that build upon and reshape yesterday's innovations to achieve a fresh, evolved design statement that characterizes the present and anticipates the future. It utilizes a current vocabulary of tastes in color, pattern, and texture, and it relies on technological advances for many of its materials and construction methods. On an upholstered, tight-seat sofa, this may mean starting with a traditional camel-back design and then exaggerating and distorting its proportions to cater to today's insistence on larger scale and more fluid lines. Instead of relying on a traditional tapestry fabric in an historic pattern, a synthetic moiré (silk) that utilizes modern technology and features a popular watery sage green palette may distinguish the contemporary furnishing from its more classic predecessors.

Contemporary design is most often clean, streamlined, and pared down. Newer design forms eschew the heavy ornamentation of the past in favor of simplicity. The clean look that is common to the design often means a preference for a neutral or monochromatic palette, one that's pure and settling. However, it can also mean the opposite: jarring primary colors slashed across the room for pure effect, or wildly graphic printed fabrics that set the room pulsating with primal rhythms.

Equally polarized, contemporary design may include either hard, geometric edges (lots of angular furni-

ture), or soft, round edges, with an abundance of serpentine, overstuffed modular seating units and gracefully curved chair and table legs.

In furniture, contemporary design sometimes explores the cutting edge with bizarre shapes that are really functional art serving as seating pieces. Other times one may find expression by merely staying current with fresh designs and materials, without going out on a futuristic limb. The look may be extremely formal, with stylistic art and furniture and elegant (but understated) fabrics, or it may run along a casual current, with simple cotton and linen upholstery coverings and casual wood and metal occasional pieces.

A room can be contemporary while still containing an antique or even several antiques—it is the overall feel that determines the style. A country checked upholstery fabric or

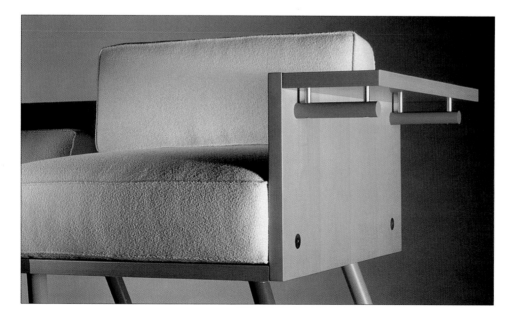

This contemporary sofa is simple, smooth, and spare. The cushions are covered in a neutral wool-blend fabric.

Wall-to-wall sisal is used as a textured floor covering in this contemporary room. The three different fabrics covering the oversized pillows bring additional texture to the room.

vintage hooked rug on the wall doesn't necessarily negate a room's contemporary style. As long as a furnishing of a different style fits into the palette and lines of the room, it doesn't much matter to which school of design it formally belongs. What matters is a consistent look and feel, not a design category. In fact, the addition of a traditional or country piece to a generally modern space can actually enhance the room's contemporary charm through contrast.

Use common sense when integrating a different design style into a contemporary space. If you fancy a traditional upholstered wing chair, select a fabric covering that's appropriate for the contemporary space—one that's a neutral, woven texture, instead of a fine damask or traditional flame stitch. Or outfit the wing chair in outrageously inappropriate attire, such as a vintage Indian blanket. The traditional chair will declare its contemporary sensibility with this unlikely match of fabric to form.

If you're a person who takes delight in things new and modern, who supports the efforts of contemporary artists and craftspersons, who appreciates a clean sweep, and who has few emotional ties to tangible vestiges of the past, then contemporary style may be the design school that's right for you.

TRADITIONAL

At the opposite extreme, if you are a person who feels most comfortable and comforted by the known, the familiar, and the time-tested, one who enjoys the refined pleasures of life in opulent, sophisticated settings, a more traditional design may be the best way for you to express your personal style. As with contemporary design, traditional can be expressed either in formal or less formal ways. But casual it is not. In its pure form, traditional design reflects the golden age of furniture—the eighteenth cen-

tury, with its dark mahogany finishes, now-classic shapes, opulent window and furniture fabrics, and the associated accoutrements of the good life. Nor is there anything primitive or remotely rustic about traditional design. In other words, if you have a penchant for putting on the Ritz, and love the fine antiques from centuries ago, traditional design is your best playground.

Traditional design is formal rather than casual. If you enjoy antiques like this gilt chair, you might enjoy working in a more traditional style.

Even traditional design can be innovative. As an alternative to parquet flooring, these oak floorboards have been stenciled in a classical pattern. The pieces feature quilting that is often seen on designer clothes.

With this design more than with most, it is important to find upholstery solutions that articulate the traditional style while still functioning to meet your day-to-day lifestyle needs. A sofa that is to be situated in a traditional-style family room may be beautiful dressed in a pale silk fabric with silk-tassel fringe trim, but it won't last a day with the kids' drinks and the cat's claws. Find a traditional woven solid or, better still, a woven print that's durable and classic, all at once. For the ultimate formal room, some of technology's newer synthetics may be a wise choice: select a

Left: Oriental carpets like the
one in this library are a
mainstay of traditional
design. The classic leather club
chairs with decorative brass
tacks evoke a distant era.

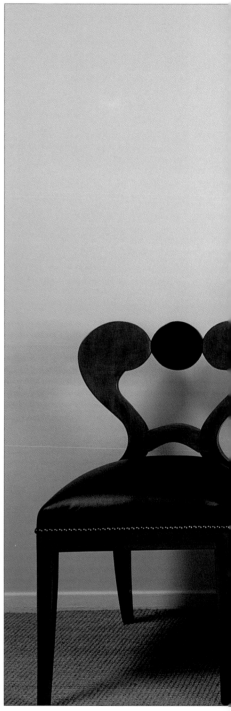

blended fabric covering that combines the look you desire with more practical functions.

In terms of selecting sofa and chair designs, traditional design is the easiest decorating arena within which to work, as it offers some clear-cut prototypes characteristic of the eighteenth century. From these, it should be an easy enough matter to select an upholstered furnishing that works for you.

The traditional color palette offers some latitude, but not as much as country, eclectic, or contemporary design. As a rule, the classic gem tones—topaz, ruby, emerald, and sapphire—dominate the traditional palette, as well as more somber, toned-down hues. Light-hearted pastels, bold primaries, and eclectic combinations of jazzy colors are not true to traditional design.

TRANSITIONAL

As you answered the questionnaire, it may have become apparent to you that you are neither entirely forward-thinking and progressive, nor entirely rooted in the past; neither a cutting-edge risk taker and trendsetter nor a traditionalist. Rather, you are probably somewhere in between. Transitional design—design that spans the bridge between contemporary and

traditional decorating—may be the generic style that feels most comfortable for you.

Because it is an in-between design—neither fish nor fowl—transitional design has some built-in flexibility. It can feature furnishings that are themselves transitional, extracting elements of traditional design and combining them with more contemporary elements. At the same time, transitional decor also can include a furnishing that is more definitively traditional—say, an upholstered wing chair, in the same space with a sleek-lined contemporary sofa. Because of this flexibility, transitional design is among the most comfortable to live in; but the trade-off is that, without a boldly declared, specific look, transitional design does not shout "style" with quite the authority of the other decorating schools.

ECLECTIC

Since the 1970s, eclecticism has emerged as a decorating style unto itself. Its recent roots in America can be traced back to the 1960s, to the societal upheaval that accompanied the Vietnam war—the anti-materialism and anti-establishment movements that were a part of the war protest. Youth began dressing differently, and their homes reflected a different sensibility as well. Beaded curtains in psychedelic colors partitioned off room spaces. Posters decorated walls as art. Suede cushions plopped right on the floor served in place of chairs. As this generation aged and itself became the establishment, it carried with it certain residuals from the prior, pivotal era: funky paintings or prints in the midst of more predictable artworks, futons instead of sofas, ethnic motifs and graphic textile prints, hand-crafted objets d'art, house plants everywhere; organic textures, and an emphasis on natural lifestyles. Thus emerged eclecticism as we know it today.

Each of us, to some degree, is eclectic. The broader our range of interests, the more eclectic we become.

The owner of this home is not afraid to combine different textures and styles. A unique two-headed lamp overlooks a more traditional striped fabric chair.

This room may look unfinished, but it is as complete as its eclectic owner wants it to be. Framed pictures are stacked against the wall while inexpensive postcards are tucked randomly along the edges of the mirror.

In personal style for the home, eclecticism is the reflection of our diverse interests and tastes, articulated under a single roof and within a single space. Rooms can range from wildly eclectic—with everything from satin buttoned traditional chairs standing elbow to elbow with director's chairs covered in canvas African prints—to more moderately eclectic, with a 1950s butterfly chair and an earlier Deco lamp gracing a contemporary room. The most eclectic spaces feature a mishmash of furnishings and

objects that defy any one period or place but gain unity through the will of the composer. In these spaces, energy is rampant, the pace is lively, and the only observable rule is "anything goes"—so long as it goes together, that is. Cultivating an eye for how to blend disparate objects takes time and experience. If this free-wheeling decorating style has appeal for you, there's no better time than the present to get started cultivating your own eye for great eclectic style.

COUNTRY

In the 1980s, the country style came onto the home decorating scene as a major player, becoming official with the launching of not one but two national (U.S.) design magazines devoted exclusively to country style. Like eclecticism, country is derived from the more natural lifestyle movement of the 1960s. It also traces its origins to the American Bicentennial and the interest in yesteryear and personal heritage that accompanied that celebration. With this renewed interest in Americana and early American furnishings, country looked to the 1700s and 1800s for its design cues, which were then interpreted to fit the present day.

Originally, country design meant a single look: dark and primitive. But by now, while it still includes that

look, it has also come to encompass a full gamut of looks that includes a dressier, sophisticated style, with a little of everything in between. On the dressy end, there's English country, which emphasizes upholstered furniture in a cheery rose or yellow palette that is charmingly frumpy. There are European expressions of country—French country, Scandinavian country, and Southern European country. There is also cottage country, with its romantic lace-and-floral grace, and contemporary country, which features new furnishings and objets d'art with elements of folk art styling.

For individuals with a nostalgic bent, who yearn for reminders of the past but eschew too much formality, country is the decorating style offering the most potential and flexibility. It is also among the most forgiving styles, allowing ample room for comfort with minimal maintenance and few opportunities for real mistakes.

Country style looks to the past for inspiration without getting too formal. This cozy cottage look is bursting with romantic florals and lace. The love seat has a down-filled cushion for added comfort.

DRESSING YOUR HOME

How you dress your home is as personal as how you dress yourself. But just as fashion do's and don'ts help you look your best, a few choice decorating guidelines ensure that your home puts its best foot forward—and that your upholstered pieces sing with style.

PATTERN

A mix of patterns can create a room that sparkles with interest. But we've all seen what happens when pattern is abused: a space that's busy, confusing, and impossible to relax in.

For the best results, limit the number of patterns to no more than five. Also, be sure there's diversity in the size of the patterns: different prints, all the same size, produce confusion. Try a large floral design on an area rug, a medium-size motif on a wall stencil, and a mini-pattern on the curtains and furniture upholstery.

Most important, keep all patterns within the same color family. When using a strong graphic pattern such as black-and-white checks, use bold solids (even red walls or rugs) as background or accents.

COLOR

As the most personal decorating choice, color must be determined entirely by what you like, not what's trendy or what someone else says looks good. If you're not sure of your favorite colors, look in your closet: your color preference will appear in your wardrobe.

It's likely that more than one color has strong appeal for you. It's okay to use different colors in different rooms, no matter what you've heard. To keep a unified visual flow from space to space, repeat some accent colors or even wall colors. Peach walls will look entirely different ac-

Do you like to wear red? This bright sofa has contrasting piping and is tempered by the patterned fabric draping the nearby table. Patterned and solid red pillows commingle on the couch.

Left: The subtle shades of these fabrics are enlivened by their textures. The bountiful window treatment shimmers, and a velvet pillow glows. A more traditional striped cotton was reserved for the classic wing chair.

cented with soft blue-gray in the bedroom and fiery coral and black in the living room. Even though the same basic color is used in both spaces, the mood couldn't be more different.

Be aware of color's effect on mood when deciding on a room's palette. Red stimulates, producing an adrenaline flow that actually heightens appetite. It's great for lively conversation in the living room, but, if you're a calorie counter, it may not be ideal for the dining room.

When lightened to a rose or pink, however, red has the opposite effect: it disarms rather than provokes, producing a conciliatory atmosphere. These are good color choices for rooms where conflicts are most often resolved.

Opposite: Paints can be applied in many different ways. These walls are barely washed in a Grecian blue that draws out the cooler tones in the tapestry sofa. A contrasting pillow avoids indulging in too much of a good thing.

Different shades of the same color have different psychological impacts. Clear yellow evokes a sunny mood, while an antique yellow connotes age and brings out more mellow feelings.

To be sure that the colors you intend to blend in a room will work together, pick up a color chart or pamphlet from a paint store or peruse a book on color. A familiarity with the principles of the color wheel will guarantee a successful mix. Most important, have a room palette in mind *before* you order upholstery fabric.

Chapter

5

FRESH FACES

LIKE EVERY OTHER TYPE OF fashion industry, the home furnishings industry is subject to certain trends and whims of the times. For upholstered furnishings, this means there are particular looks that are especially popular from one decade to the next—both in the shape of the furniture and in the appearance and type of fabrics that cover it. While trends do change from season to season, the predominant ones are carried forward from one year to the next, characterizing an entire decade more than an individual year.

As in the fashion apparel industry, home furnishing manufacturers rely on small changes from season to season to encourage sales. This practice caters to consumers with a desire to stay on top of the newest and hottest trends, who are willing to chuck all or some of their existing furniture for new pieces that are up-to-the-minute. There are two major home furnishing markets each year in America, both taking place in High Point, North Carolina—one in the spring and the other in the fall. As a result, manufacturers introduce a few new styles and innovations twice each year. Sometimes, the furniture making its debut at these shows is an entirely new line of pieces, while at other times it is merely an addition to an existing line. No reasonable consumer, however trend-oriented, can

possibly keep up. And there's really no good reason to. Most of the biannual introductions are only slight variations on what's been available before. If regional heritage (reproduction) pieces have been in demand for a couple of years, each season may introduce furnishings from yet another region—nothing exactly new, just more of the same.

The biggest movement for change from one season to the next occurs in the arena of color. Furniture manufacturers are always trying to introduce variations of a popular color, or to promote an entirely different color, at each new furniture market. Some

The home furnishings industry often takes its cues from fashion. This room is filled with neutrals and nature-inspired prints. Color is the most significant change you'll see from one season to the next.

of the colors "take," becoming staples in the decade's decorating palette, while others don't get quite as warm a reception and all but disappear from the showroom floors and sample swatches a season or two later.

You don't have to be a home furnishings expert or insider to predict what will appear at the next season's market. You only have to realize that the home furnishings industry takes its cues from the fashion apparel industry, then stay abreast of what's happening in apparel. The colors, fabrics, shapes, and relative formality of clothes presented by the fashion designers and manufacturers one season will inevitably influence the look

of home furnishings presented at that industry's major markets the following season.

For consumers interested in purchasing upholstered pieces that will offer lasting style, now is a good time to buy. Certain movements in apparel fashion are proving to have staying power, and their counterparts in home furnishings are too. Practical-minded consumers will be relieved to know that the two most resounding buzzwords in both industries are "casual" and "comfortable." When it comes to purchasing upholstered furniture, nothing could be more sensible or reassuring.

The desire for home furnishings that are both casual and comfortable is something that designers and consumers definitely agree on.

CASUAL

We've all seen the advertisement: designer Ralph Lauren in faded blue jeans photographed next to a battered pick-up truck. The message is clear: you don't have to drive a Mercedes or Lexus and wear Armani suits to have style. More and more Americans (and Europeans) are learning that it's okay to approach life realistically, dressing our bodies and our homes to fit our casual lifestyles, with fewer and fewer hang-ups and pretensions.

A comparative glance at decorating magazines from the eighties and nineties confirms this. Style in interior designs, including upholstered furnishings, for the 1980s was more heavily oriented toward appearance than lifestyle. Upholstered chairs and sofas of the eighties were covered in fabrics that wouldn't endure many spills or scratches. The forms of the furnishings weren't configured to fit the human body in various postures of relaxation, but were designed mainly to look good. All that, thankfully, has changed. And this welcome change promises to remain in force well into the next century.

"Decorating was 'pretend' in the eighties," says New York designer Lyn Peterson of Motif Designs. "Now we're secure enough to furnish our homes with things that are our own personal biography. It's a casual approach I call 'real-life decorating,'" she says.

"We want real-life solutions. We no longer want homes as shrines to decorating, but as answers to how we live," the designer continues. She cites a photograph in a nineties decorating magazine as proof. It used to be that rooms featured in magazines showed few signs of human habitation. In today's magazines, evidence of living people is everywhere. "We're not afraid to show the reading lamps, the bag of clothes being returned to Bloomingdale's, the kids' school knapsacks, the TVs."

For upholstered furnishings, creating a casual style means avoiding

matching fabrics on all pieces within a space. Just as the trend in apparel fashion is toward mix-and-match, so is it in dressing the home's most comfortable seating pieces.

In the 1980s, style was more important in home design than lifestyle. This white room is elegant, but not practical for everyone.

"Casual is an eclectic mix," says Larry Shaw, president of Currey & Company, which creates individual accent pieces for stores such as L.L. Bean, Eddie Bauer, Pottery Barn, and Crate and Barrel. "Casual means feeling free to tastefully mix inherited pieces or even furnishings from your old apartment with new pieces," he adds.

Older upholstered pieces may not have the look you want, appearing dated by the fabric's palette, print, or fiber content. But with the new movement toward casual style, the old furnishing no longer has to be discarded. It can be salvaged, given an entirely fresh look by taking it to an upholsterer to be re-covered in a more current fabric of your choice.

"Sometimes this panics furniture manufacturers," Shaw concedes, "but that's how I define the new relaxed attitude in decorating. It's rooms that can evolve over time."

As a designer, Peterson agrees with Shaw. "By definition, casual is 'happening by chance; fortuitous.' In decorating, casual does happen by chance. It's by chance that you have the trunk your father brought back from Vietnam or the sofa you found on the curb or the dining room table your mother gave you."

Right: A more casual room invites you to relax among its pillows.

Left: Casual upholstered furniture is available from manufacturers, but don't be afraid to recover a flea-market find in new fabrics.

Peterson, along with other de-signers, encourages consumers to rid themselves of their ingrained tendency to eschew the curb or flea-market find. Some of the best sofa and chair shapes are found in these unlikely places, needing only a little spiffing up with new upholstery or slipcovers.

Short of recycling old, inherited, or second-hand pieces, casual upholstered furniture is available in abundance from a plethora of major furniture manufacturers and reputable retailers. Peterson recommends looking at the casual lines from Thomasville, Ethan Allen, the Bombay Company, and Hitchcock Chair. Other designers add Broyhill, Lane, Lexington, La-Z-Boy, and Crate and Barrel to the list.

Casual upholstered furniture does not have to be inexpensive or in any way connote a lower quality. It

Below: Casual can still be elegant. This traditional leather sofa is made more casual with the toss of a kilim pillow.

can be upscale, too. "'Casual elegance' are the words you're hearing," says designer Raymond Waites of Gear. "I still have my country table, but I'm using Victorian silver on it instead of jam jars. It's the tension that exists between old and new, deluxe and homespun, that leads to this new casual quality."

For upholstered pieces, casual elegance might mean dressing a pedigree eighteenth-century chair or a Victorian settee in a contemporary, all-natural-fiber, unbleached woven fabric. Or it could mean the opposite: taking a generic street-side find, then dressing it to the hilt. The idea is that nothing is so precious that it can't be used in a real-life home environment.

Casual furniture isn't only wicker or iron frames upholstered in casual fabrics, "but furniture that evokes good memories," adds Shaw. "Often, the product isn't pristine but has imperfections that give it a used look that tells a story." Sometimes, the used look is deliberate—and new. Chenille coverings, which are reminiscent of grandmother's house, are one example.

Other examples include Waites' two new collections of furniture: his New Country Gear collection, which has a rustic log-cabin feel, and his Gear Collection, with its more dressed-up Monticello antecedent. The country designs are made of pine with a rough-hewn, old quality. Even the more classic ash furniture line features "an imperfect quality to the finish so that, if it's abused, it's very forgiving," Waites explains.

His new collections tell a story of America's past, as do country lines from such manufacturers as Lane and Lexington. "But country isn't the only kind of casual furniture," insists Peterson. "Casual also means the contemporary sectional sofa that you can reconfigure to fit your needs."

More than referring to any one furniture or design style, casual is all about an attitude. "It's being able to do what your mother told you never to do—to put your feet up on the coffee table or the sofa," declares Shaw. Casual style means homes that are meant to be lived in and enjoyed for their relaxed qualities.

Casual is more a state of mind than one specific style. Even fine antiques have a place in casual design. Above: A rolled chaise lounge that's meant to be used, not just admired. Right: Beautiful daybeds easily toss off their decorative pillows when they're called into use.

WHAT'S GOOD FOR THE BODY...

FOR AN INSIDE TRACK ON THE hottest new casual upholstered furniture fabrics, stop by the Gap. Or thumb through the fashion pages of an Eddie Bauer or L.L. Bean catalog. Nearly every major furniture manufacturer has picked up on consumers' demand to dress their furniture in the same relaxed, casual way they clothe their bodies.

"We define casual as how we spend our leisure time, whether it be in furniture or clothing," says Sandra White, director of advertising at Bernhardt, a furniture company. "That means we're upholstering our furniture in the same fabrics we put on our bodies."

With thirteen colors of denim and three colors (green, brown, and natural) of 100 percent natural cotton, Bernhardt's "Ready for Wear" fabric program reflects the correlation between furniture and fashion. "The language is the same for both—washable, wearable, mix and match, pattern on pattern," says White.

A slipcover look using pre-washed cotton is furniture manufacturing company Pearson's response to the trend. "We're also combining more than one fabric on a frame,

the way you would dress yourself," says Pearson's Elizabeth Marvin, design assistant in fabrics. "On

Mixing prints and patterns on one piece of furniture is becoming more popular. Top: Chintz, vintage florals, and needlepoint pillows blossom side by side. Bottom: Striped, checked, and patterned fabrics share the spotlight.

one sofa, we used a pinstripe denim and two other correlating denims."

Broyhill's Don Essenberg has reservations about too much mixing of prints on a single piece, however. "While you are seeing what we call 'collage' sofas—sofas with a border in one fabric, the top in another, the skirt in a different one, and arm and back pillows in yet a different print—I don't see a lot of people dressing that way. I have to wonder how long it will last," he says.

More typical, and promising, Essenberg believes, is the trend in mixing three fabrics on a sofa—one for the body fabric, with two additional fabrics covering two pairs of throw pillows. This, he believes, is closer to how people dress, accessorizing in accent prints, rather than putting together different prints on the body of a shirt or dress.

Identifying other top-selling furniture coverings is like glancing inside your closet. All of the weekend clothing fabrics—rugby stripes, plaids, flannels, and checks—are represented in furniture upholstery fabrics. The result is a relaxed look that takes the starched seams out of interior design, making it more user-friendly than ever before.

COMFORT

S ECOND ONLY TO "CASUAL," "comfortable" is the buzzword reflecting a major trend in upholstered furniture. It means two things: furnishings that function well to fit your lifestyle, and furnishings that feel good to the body.

As part of an entire room setting, today's upholstered furnishings must fit into a decorating scheme that has comfort as its underlying core. San Francisco designer Agnes Bourne likes to talk about her profession as "a healing art" (a term she borrowed from another designer). "Comfort has a lot to do with design as a healing art because it takes the aggravation out of your world," she explains. "It starts by organizing your home to support you in what you do."

If you habitually sprawl onto the sofa to watch television or read, having to remove a lot of throw pillows or re-fluff down cushions each time quickly becomes a nuisance. "It's like putting on your underwear backwards every day," says Bourne. "It's a needless aggravation."

To ensure comfort, she recommends making a list of what makes you uncomfortable, then redesigning, refurnishing, or reupholstering to rid yourself of unnecessary annoyances.

A large sectional sofa functions well in comfortable design, and its ample cushions feel good, too.

How a furnishing functions is paramount to how much comfort it will provide. "If you like to lie down on your sofa, one with a tuxedo arm is terrible. It's not comfortable; a rolled arm is," observes Lyn Peterson.

Similarly, if you enjoy having a dozen friends over to watch the Super Bowl, a conventional sofa won't be comfortable because it won't function to meet your needs; a sectional will, says Kathe Waskin, an Annapolis designer. She also warns that, if your family includes pets and children, "hands-off furniture won't be comfortable, either."

In addition to functioning well, comfortable design is characterized by furniture that feels good to the body. For many furniture manufacturers, today's solution is larger, more generous proportions to better accommodate relaxation. Bernhardt's answer, for example, is the chair-and-a-half: "It gives you that 'cuddle up' potential. You can fit two people on it, or one—with plenty of room to slouch," explains Sandra White.

How upholstered pieces are constructed plays a major role in how comfortable they feel to the body. "Once you have eight-way hand-tied construction on a sofa, comfort follows," says White.

Peterson offers consumers some tips on how to ensure comfort beyond insisting on certain construction methods and materials. "Don't just sit on a sofa when you're shopping; lie down on it," she recommends. "Certain pillows will pitch you forward when you lie down. Down filling is only good for back cushions, not seat cushions. It leaves an imprint few of us want to be remembered by."

Waskin also warns against furniture cushions stuffed entirely with down. Instead, she recommends a combination of down and polyester fibers. "Down has to be fluffed, and, having to work in your room is not comfortable," she says. "A down-poly combination gives you the comfort of down plus springback action."

Comfort ultimately is about designing to your needs, not to a look. "When you design to your needs, you honor yourself," concludes Bourne. "This produces comfort."

To ensure a comfortable home, create a look that meets your needs. It's important to consider the materials and construction methods used in upholstered pieces, however. This room is striking, but it may not be suited to everyone's lifestyle.

COMFORT IS MORE THAN SKIN deep, going beyond the purely physical appeal of a plush sofa or cushy chair. Good design addresses a psychological dimension of comfort, as well. Color is one of the most important vehicles for reaching this.

Studies prove that color not only is a matter of visual preference, but also has a profound impact on mood. One color can elevate spirits, while another can depress them. Each color, down to its precise shades and tones, has a different effect on the human psyche.

In choosing color wisely for upholstered furnishings, keep in mind some of the effects hues have on mood. Determine what kind of mood you want established in a living space, then select colors accordingly. Also keep in mind your own personality: If you're a hothead, you'd best avoid red. If you're meek and need stimulation and encouragement to bring out your personality to the fullest, red may be the ideal answer for your upholstered pieces. A paler tone of red, a blush or pink, on the other hand, has an entirely different impact on mood, working to soothe ruffled feelings and create a conciliatory spirit.

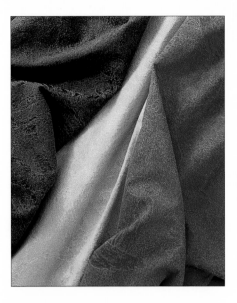

Most people would agree that color can affect mood. In addition to fiber content, consider which colors you like to be surrounded by and the mood you're trying to create before selecting fabrics.

Agnes Bourne illustrates the point further. "There are all kinds of white, but some are depressing and others are uplifting," she says. "White with a touch of violet uplifts, while white with a tint of green may not leave you feeling as well. White toned with yellow may be depressing because it feels aged," she explains.

In addition to influencing and altering mood, colors are extremely personal. Chosen well, they can be as comforting as a favorite book on a rainy day. "People really do have certain colors they enjoy more than others, and living with them is comforting," says Bourne.

The colors you wear most often are the colors that will comfort you in your home, on upholstered furnishings. But, perhaps you wear black because you live in New York and that color happens to express New York chic, but you also love looking at red. "Even if you wear black all the time yet you enjoy looking at red, think about introducing red in your home," suggests Bourne.

"Your home is like a stage," she concludes. "You can consciously create the ambiance you want. Comfort is all about designing from the inside out."

Chapter

6

A GLOSSARY OF MATERIALS, TERMS, AND TECHNIQUES

ACETATE

Acetate is a cellulose fiber that features wood pulp as its major raw ingredient. It is more commonly used for window treatment fabrics than upholstery coverings, because of its good draping characteristics. However, it is frequently used in blends to make satins and brocades, which do appear on more formal upholstered furnishings. Negative features of acetate that prevent its use by itself, without some other fiber, include heat sensitivity, absorbency, a tendency to shrink and lose shape when wet, and low durability.

ACRYLICS

Related to polyester and nylon, acrylic fibers are made from fossil fuels. Acrylics are desirable in a blended fabric due to their texture—they have the soft feel, durability, and warmth of wool—plus the fact that they are resistant to stretch, easily retaining their shape. Unlike wool, acrylics also have the advantage of being mothproof, and they can be lightly sponged to remove light stains. On the down side, acrylics are heat-sensitive. Dralon

Chintz is printed cotton with a surface glaze.

velvet is perhaps the most common fabric blend made using acrylics. In addition to Dralon, trade names acrylics are found under include Acrilan, Orlon, Teklon, and Courtelle.

CHINTZ

First used during the William and Mary period, chintz is a printed cotton fabric that usually has been glazed. Most commonly found in floral patterns, it is indelibly linked to the English country style, used on both furnishing upholsteries and draperies as a hallmark communicating the look associated with that school of design. Chintz does not refer to a specific traditional weave—the fabric is a plain weave woven on a plain loom—but to the surface treatment of the material once it has been woven. Because the pattern is printed onto the woven material instead of actually being a part of the weave, it is subject to fading from sunlight and does not offer the durability of a fabric with the pattern woven in. The glazed finish may wear off over time. (Chintz's frequent inclusion under weaves is technically inaccurate, but is due to its common misconception as a weave instead of as a fabric type.)

COTTON

Cotton is a vegetable fiber from the cotton plant that, with our growing environmental awareness, is experiencing a burgeoning popularity. Cotton fabric is durable and strong. Its texture and weight can be

100 percent cotton

colorfast, if of good quality, making them washable without requiring dry cleaning. Various finishes can be applied, including those to make the fabric resistant to shrinkage, stains, and wrinkles. All-cotton fabrics can be given a permanent press finish that ensures low maintenance. All-natural, undyed cottons are especially in demand today.

Textured linen

adapted to create a variety of fabric types, from light voiles, chintzes, and cotton satins to heavier corduroys. Glazing (as with chintzes) can be added for a different look, as well as one that resists soiling. Cottons take dye easily and are typically

CUPRO

The cellulose fiber known as cupro is similar to viscose rayon, but it has two distinct advantages: it is stronger and it can be fashioned into finer yarns. Its use is restricted largely to fabric blends that make good lining materials.

LINEN

A dressier cousin to cotton, linen comes from the vegetable fiber of the flax plant. Like cotton, it is strong and durable (and even stronger when wet), but it has some drawbacks: unless treated, it is extremely prone to wrinkling and creasing. Its use is not advised for damp areas, such as a three-season porch or drafty basement, as it is subject to mildewing in damp conditions. For persons interested in adding textural interest to the home through upholstery fabric, linen is a good choice, as it can feature rich textures that intrigue the eye without the need for a printed pattern. Left in a neutral palette, linen is a common choice for contemporary or transitional interiors, where its sub-

Cupro is stronger than rayon.

tle suggestion of pattern through texture makes a desired understatement, but with the unmistakable feel of quality. Used in a blend with other materials or given a crease-resistant finish, some of linen's wrinkling proclivity can be reduced. Linen is typically more expensive than the other natural-plant fiber, cotton.

MODACRYLICS

The next generation in the processing procedure after acrylics, modacrylics are valued in blends with natural or other manmade fibers.

MODAL

A modified rayon, this fiber looks like cotton and has similar properties. It is made from cotton waste or wood and is used in fabric blends to upgrade or offset some of the weaker characteristics of the natural or other synthetic fibers present in the blend.

NYLON

Also derived from petroleum (which may pose an insurmountable obstacle to the most planet-conscious consumers), nylon, like polyester, is typically used in a blended fabric

Modacrylics are the next generation of acrylics.

rather than by itself for an upholstery covering. Its inherent strength and wrinkle resistance make its addition desirable. But unlike polyester, nylon is highly absorbent, making it less stain-resistant. In addition, it is heat-sensitive, which means that it tends to fade or discolor when exposed to too much sunlight. When a blended fabric consists of a sizable percentage of nylon, care should be taken to situate the upholstered furnishing out of direct sunlight. Some of the lighter-weight nylons are unsuitable as upholstery fabrics. Because of its stretching ability, nylon is an easy material to use for conforming to the compound curves of certain chair shapes. Nylon is currently produced

under a range of trademarked names (Celon, Bri-nylon, Perlon, and Enkalon, among others). Your fabric or furniture supplier should be able to identify the material as nylon.

POLYESTER

Given a brutal rap during the era of polyester leisure suits in men's fashion, polyester is not necessarily the bad guy it's commonly portrayed to be. Used in a fabric blend with natural fibers, its processed nature as a material that is chemically produced from petroleum derivatives is not glaringly obvious; instead of looking "fake," polyester, in a blend, can take a low profile, allowing the natural fiber to dominate the textile's appearance. Although a 100 percent polyster fabric is never desirable when a natural, organic look is the

Nylon in rich patterns

goal, polyester can be used with natural fibers to achieve a more utilitarian, longer-lasting, lower-maintenance product. Polyester does not stretch (which can be a problem in certain upholstery treatments), is fast-drying, and has low absorbency—features important to a textile that's apt to undergo heavy use in the home as an upholstery fabric. In addition, polyester is strong, making the blended fabric less likely to puncture or tear. Because of its light weight, however, its use for upholstery coverings is necessarily restricted to blends. Trade names include Terylene, Tergal, and Terlenka.

Brilliant silk velvets offer luxurious options in upholstery fabrics.

RAYON

Rayon was among the first manmade cellulose fibers. These days, however, with so many variations of manmade fibers being produced, fiber contents usually won't specify rayon, but one or more of the particular man-made types, such as acetate, viscose, or cupro, among others.

SILK

Long relegated to formal rooms, silk is now being used to add an elegant touch in a variety of interior designs other than eighteenth-century-style traditional settings. Hand-dyed in rich, abstract colorations, or left in a natural-looking neutral to work with a monochromatic room palette, it is appearing with increasing frequency in contemporary design schemes.

Unblended silk fabric is 100 percent natural animal fiber extracted from the cocoons of the silkworm larvae. Although silk fabrics are strong and resilient and not easily prone to wrinkling or creasing, they do not withstand heat well. As upholstery on a furnishing located in front of a sunny window, they are probably not the ideal textile choice, as they are

Polyester takes many forms.

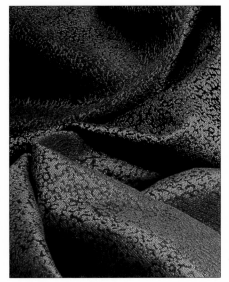

Shimmering rayon

weakened by sunlight. In terms of luster, silk, with its shiny, watery look, is without peer. Its fine finish is also unsurpassed for showing coloration, whether subtle or intense. However, most dyes used on silk are not colorfast, and dry cleaning is therefore usually recommended, increasing the required maintenance of an upholstered piece. (Forget easy wipe-up of stain-causng spills.) For furnishings subject to frequent use, especially in homes with young children or pets, all-silk upholstery is not recommended due to the high maintenance needed.

TRIACETATE

This cellulose fiber is popular in blends because of its resilience, nonabsorbency, and heat-resistance.

Viscose rayon is usually blended with cotton or linen.

It is featured in mixes with both natural or other man-made fibers.

VISCOSE RAYON

This is a regenerated vegetable fiber that is chemically made, involving the processing of wood pulp. On their own, viscose rayons aren't a likely upholstery choice: they are not durable, strong, shrink-resistant, fray-free, mothproof, or static-free. To overcome these handicaps, various treatments of the fabric are necessary. When blended with cotton or linen yarns, viscose rayon fabrics have satisfactory wear. Viscose rayons also are among the least expensive of fibers, making them a common choice in blends. They are also easy to work with. In addition, the fiber is especially suited for simulating silk. Though used often in upholstery fabric blends, viscose rayon's most important use isn't as an upholstery fabric, but as a draping material.

WOOL

An all-natural animal fiber made from the coats of sheep or goats, wool is valued for its insulating warmth. As a choice for chilly rooms, it is unsurpassed in comfort. Because of its warm look and feel, wool is also a pleasing complement

Colorful wools are durable coverings.

to the "lodge look" (the Adirondack camp style) that has become popular in interior design over the past few seasons. Naturally absorbent, wool can retain body heat—a plus for cooler spaces in winter—but on the down side, it also absorbs spills. A stain-resistant treatment can overcome problems associated with its absorbency. Two other problems are incumbent with wool as a fabric upholstery, however: it is subject to shrinkage and to attack by moths. Both dilemmas can be averted by making sure the fabric has been properly treated, either pre-shrunk or made shrink-resistant, and made mothproof. Wool's tendency to feel scratchy to the skin can be overcome by selecting a predominantly wool fabric that's blended with another, more gentle fiber.

TYPES OF WEAVE

A Dobby weave produces intricate patterns and textures.

weave, the movement of the shuttle across the warp threads is dictated by the use of punched cards.

LENO WEAVE

Also known as gauze weave, this technique features a lacy, open combination of yarns made by twisting warp yarns around each other in figure eights, as the weft yarn moves between them.

DOBBY WEAVE

A special weave, this one incorporates a complex Dobby loom to produce such motifs and textures as intricate geometrics that reappear at consistent places throughout the weave. Dobby repeats are small and use a limited number of "healds" (frames that raise the warp yarns).

JACQUARD WEAVE

A fancy weave, Jacquard fabrics were introduced by Joseph Jacquard in 1801, when he invented a special loom for the weaving of figured fabrics. Jacquards include self-colored designs, as well as designs woven from two or more yarn colors. The most delicate and ornamental woven patterns available in upholstery fabrics will have been created on a Jacquard loom. In a Jacquard

A fancy Jacquard weave fabric

An example of a pile weave

PILE WEAVE

This is a weave in which a pile is created by using two warp threads, one to form the base fabric while the other is pulled up above the base and cut off to produce a pile. The most obvious examples of pile upholstery fabrics are velvet and corduroy. In upholstering a piece of furniture, it's important to make sure the pile runs in the same direction on all parts of the furnishing. Otherwise, a difference in coloration will result, much as it does when a vaccuum cleaner is pulled in different directions along various stretches of a pile carpet.

Satin weave fabric has a smooth surface.

Plain weave fabrics come in many colors and patterns.

PLAIN WEAVE

This is the simplest, most affordable, and most common fabric weave. It can be used in one or more colors and with different types and thicknesses of yarn. When contrasting or different colors are used for the warp and weft, the product is known as "shot" fabric.

SATIN WEAVE

This weave simply refers to one in which more warp thread is revealed on the surface of the fabric than in a plain weave. The result is an extremely smooth, lustrous surface.

TWILL WEAVE

A common term in clothing, twill refers to the diagonal, ridged pattern created by this type of weave. The effects will vary, according to the weight of the yarn and the direction of the ridging. The classic herringbone pattern is a variation on twill weaving.

Barkweave is named for its rough texture.

Brocades are woven using silk yarns.

BARKWEAVE

This self-colored woven fabric features a texture that imitates the roughness of tree bark. It is typically woven from cotton fibers.

BROCADE

Brocade is traditional and extremely decorative weave created on a Jacquard loom using silk yarns. Its pattern repeat is much smaller, and therefore it appears more intricate, than that of a Jacquard damask. Brocade is not recommended for furnishings undergoing frequent or heavy use, as it is more fragile than damask. First entering popularity as an upholstery fabric during the William and Mary period, brocade was then imported from France by the yard.

BROCATELLE

Woven on a Jacquard loom, brocatelle features a raised pattern created from silk yarns in a satin weave, which gives it an embossed look. It is believed to have been originally created to emulate fine hand-tooled Italian leather.

Brocatelle's embossed pattern is created from silk yarns using a satin weave.

CANVAS

Canvas is one of the strongest and most durable fabrics available. Also known as duck, it is a closely woven material, usually made of linen, hemp, or cotton.

CHAMBRAY

A close relative of denim, this woven cotton or cotton-blend fabric also receives its primary look from the use of colored warp yarns with white weft yarns. But unlike denim, chambray can include self-patterning—figuring, stripes, and other designs.

CHENILLE

Remembered by baby boomers as the bedspreads at grandmother's house, chenille is now being used as

Damask comes in silk and cotton.

an upholstery fabric. It is a heavily textured pile material, in which the fuzzy yarns in the weft produce the decorative, soft pile. It is most often woven from cotton and/or manmade fibers.

CORDUROY

Featuring a pile weave, corduroy is a ribbed fabric woven so that the ribs run the length of the cloth, in the direction of the warp. As with velvet, the look or shading of the material will appear different unless the brush of the pile has been uniformly applied to the upholstered piece. Corduroys entered into popularity with the Victorian era, and they have experienced a renewed interest today, taking on a distinctly more casual look with a longer pile.

DAMASK

Woven on a Jacquard loom from silk, damask is a light upholstery fabric with a usually complex design whose repeat pattern is generally large-

Today's chenilles are woven from cotton or synthetic fibers.

scale. The background of the design is created with a satin weave, making the fabric reversible (the reverse side's design is in alternate shades from that on the front of the material). For the restoration of period pieces, silk damask is the correct material, having come into popular use with the Adam period. Cotton damasks also are available as upholstery fabrics, and at a lower cost.

However, the weave of the cottons is less intricate than that using silk yarns, and the fiber is not authentic to period furnishings.

DENIM

Created using a durable twill weave, usually from cotton or cotton-blend fibers, the unique look that is denim is produced by colored warp yarns and white weft yarns. Denim, long popular in casual fashions, is now one of the hottest upholstery fabrics on the market, catering to the trend toward casual comfort.

FOLKWEAVE

This is a coarse, loosely woven fabric typically made from cotton fibers, then printed with a checked or striped pattern. The number of long warp float yarns results in easy snagging, making this fabric unsuitable for tight upholstery coverings.

GINGHAM

Undergoing renewed popularity with the country design movement, gingham is an old-fashioned woven fabric that is lightweight and usually made from washable cotton. Its pattern of checks (or sometimes stripes) is woven into the fabric, usually in a combination of colored yarns with white.

HANDWOVEN EMBROIDERY

One of the most customized upholstery materials, fabrics stitched in petit point or gros point typically are made to fit a particular furnishing. Usually embroidered with wool yarns, these fabrics often have a

Beautiful hand embroidery makes an elegant fabric.

Moiré is traditionally woven from silk.

coordinating or matching unembroidered fabric stitched to them to produce a size appropriate for upholstery work. When purchasing a handwoven embroidered furnishing, be sure that the embroidery work is squared up for a balanced look.

MATELASSÉ

One of the most coveted textiles for bed coverings on the market today, matelassé is a cotton, rayon, or silk fabric with raised patterns woven into it in a single color. The design (usually floral) can be seen only in relief, from its embossed appearance. The fabric is now being used as a slipcover material or as an upholstery fabric in its own right.

MOIRÉ

Traditionally woven from silk to have a finely ribbed texture with a watery design, moiré can be found in synthetic form today. When made of pure silk, it is a formal, fragile fabric, and should be used accordingly.

MUSLIN

This plain-weave fabric is an important one to be familiar with when engaging in commissioning or do-it-yourself upholstery work. Originally made in Mosul, an ancient city in Mesopotamia, muslin—either bleached or unbleached—is a material frequently used as a first covering on custom-upholstered furnishings. It is a lightweight,

open-textured cotton cloth sold under names such as batiste, lawn, and nainsook.

REPP

A hard-working weave, repp is a plain worsted or cotton fabric with fine lines running along the weft of the cloth. It is noted for its soil-resistance and durability.

SATIN

Another fine material used primarily for formal upholstered pieces, satin features a lustrous weave made from silk yarns. While it is functional for covering a flat seat back, it is not recommended for any tufted work or any upholstery treatment involving buttoning. The fabric will not lie properly in pleats when buttoned down, due to the silky nature of the material. An alternative form of the traditional satin weave is "slub" satin. This is also a sheer fabric, like traditional satin weave, but its smooth surface is deliberately interrupted by broken, uneven places in the weave formed by "slubs" in the weft, making the fabric less sheer than traditional satin.

TOILE DE JOUY

Related to chintz, toile is a second type of plain-woven printed cotton (not a traditional weave per se, but rather the printed treatment represented on a plain weave). It originated in France during the reign of Louix XVI. Its printed scenes depicted the life of the times—especially voyages or exotic landscapes. It is used to upholster French (or any period and provenance of antique) furniture, in addition to being a favorite historic reproduction for wallcoverings and window treatments.

Toile de Jouy is perfect on a period piece.

TAFFETA

Originally made from silk but now frequently available from a weave of synthetic fibers, taffeta is a close-weave fabric featuring a subtle weft-facing rib.

TAPESTRY

Tapestry is a woven fabric that usually employs coarse, multicolored yarns. It is, however, available in various weights, suitable for different needs (heavier weights will be warmer and less fragile to sit on). As a medium to work with—a factor to consider if having upholstery or re-upholstery work commissioned—medium to light weights are the easiest to use; heavier tapestries can pose problems in pleating and machining that can lead to less than superior workmanship and an unsatisfactory final product. Often, tapestries are reproductions of original hand-woven historic patterns, but contemporary designs are also available. When an antique or hand-crafted look is desired, they are a good selection.

Colorful tapestry

GLOSSARY

·141·

TWEED

This heavy fabric, familiar from the clothing industry, is made in hand-woven effects of (usually) wool, in combination with cotton or synthetics.

VELVET

Constructed with a pile weave, velvet, in its original form, used only silk yarns. Today, many velvets are blends or consist of entirely man-made fibers. In its traditional application, velvet is used as upholstery with the brush of the pile running downward on the inside and outside backs, downward on the inside and outside arms, and forward on the seats. This ensures that the pile runs in the same direction throughout the furnishing to provide consistent coloration. Today, however, in order to reduce costs, the application technique is different. To avoid joining the fabric, the brush of the pile is run sideways across the upholstered pieces. This results in the shading looking different on the piece's different sides. When having antique pieces re-upholstered, consider an antique figured velvet for such early furnishings as wing chairs and Knole settees. For Victorian furnishings, the period-correct velvet is mohair, which has a stiffer pile than normal velvet. As a woolen weave, mohair must be treated for protection against moths.

Velvets were originally silk. Today, blends and manmade velvets are popular.

SPRINGS

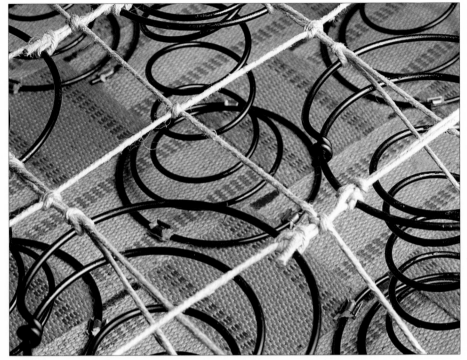

Double-cone coil springs

PILLOW SPRINGS

Made of small-gauge wire, these are the springs that are used on seated pieces' backs and arms. They resemble coil seat springs except that they are knotted at each end and are a lighter weight.

SINGLE CONE SPRINGS

Unlike double-cone springs, these have a different shape, large at the top and narrow at the base; they look like one half of a double-cone spring.

DOUBLE-CONE COIL SPRINGS

This is the best quality of spring for sofas and large chairs for which a deep, comfortable, resilient seat is desired—and it's also the most expensive. Made of heavy coiled metal, these seat springs are shaped like an hour-glass, larger at either end and smaller in the middle. They are available in various degrees of compression, including soft, medium, and hard, determined by the size of the center coil. If the center coil is wide, the spring will be soft. Wider centers for soft and medium seats are the most commonly used. (For especially heavy persons, hard springs with small centers are desirable.)

NO-SAG SPRINGS

Made from continuous wire shaped in a zigzag, no-sag springs are popular for mass-produced furnishings because of their reduction of required man-hours and subsequently more affordable price points.

SPRING BARS

Made up of either three or four conical springs attached at their ends to a metal bar or support, spring bars are used primarily on lower-end furnishings, as their presence eliminates the need for the time-consuming practice of attaching webbing and stitching the springs in place. The ends of the bar are secured on top of the seat rail for a rigid-edged seat. Although spring bars may result in less sagging than does webbing, they are less resilient and therefore less comfortable than a different type of spring that requires webbing.

STUFFINGS

ALVA

No longer in commercial use as a filling, alva, a type of seaweed, was a favorite first (underneath) stuffing on Victorian upholstery.

COTTON FLOCK

Now obsolete, cotton flock was popular in Victorian times as a top filling over a base filling of alva. It flattens quickly, has a short lifespan, and is not suitable for reuse.

DOWN

A favorite material for bed pillows and comforters, down also is considered a luxury stuffing for upholstered furnishings. It consists of the feathers from young birds, or the light, fluffy undercoating, on which there is no quill shaft, from older ducks, geese, and other water fowl. More resilient than feathers, down stuffing tends to leave a body imprint on the seat, which requires fluffing and reshaping—a maintenance feature some consumers choose to avoid, even at the loss of the more comfortable seat.

FEATHERS

Taken from geese, ducks, water fowl, or poultry, feathers of one type of bird or a mixture of them are used as upholstery stuffings. Poultry feathers are the lowest quality. Unlike down, feathers tend to flatten and become heavy when sat upon, with the seated furnishing losing its plumpness because of the stuffing's low resiliency. Feather cushions require frequent fluffing—more frequent even than down.

FOAM RUBBER

One of the most expensive and best stuffings for new upholstered furnishings, foam rubber is rubber that contains air bubbles. It is available

Hair from horses, cattle, and hogs was once popular as a filling. Today it is reserved for custom work.

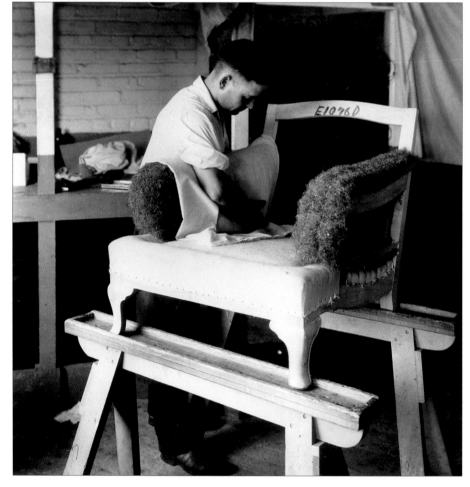

in slab form for use as a stuffing material, or in molded form as cushion units. Classic foam rubber tends to break down and granulate over time, and is no longer widely available, having been replaced by the newer high-resiliency (HR) polyurethane foam, which does not deteriorate.

HAIR

One of the most popular upholstery stuffing materials before the advent of foam rubber and synthetic materials, the curled hair from horses, cattle, or hogs is now restricted to custom upholstery work, especially that on antiques. It is considered the best type of loose filling available, but its price (especially for the labor involved) is prohibitive.

KAPOK

This silky fiber from the seed pods of silk, cotton, or the kapok tree is soft and fluffy, lending itself well to use as a stuffing material for cushions and pillows.

MOSS

Dried and shredded, plant moss forms a resilient stuffing material for upholstered furniture—and it is moth-resistant.

Filling gives shape to a chair.

PALM FIBER

Made from the shredded leaves of Algerian palm trees, palm fiber is a good foundation material for upholstered furnishings and is more desirable than tow. It has good resilience and durability because it is processed in a manner similar to that used on hair, giving it bulk and springiness.

SHODDY

Also known as rag flock, this material is a low-grade filling sometimes used in upholstery. It is manufactured by reducing waste wool or cotton textiles to their original fiber form. Seldom used alone, shoddy is more commonly seen as part of a layered filling.

TOW

A flax plant fiber, tow is firm, inexpensive, and easy to work with. On the down side, it is not very resilient. Its chief use in upholstery is as a firm foundation (first stuffing) for more resilient stuffing materials.

TULA FIBER

Grown in the southwestern United States, this fiber is coated with rubber for a strong stuffing material; it has a spongy appearance.

WEBBING AND FOUNDATION MATERIALS

BOTTOMING

As the word indicates, this is the muslin cover tacked to the under-side of an upholstered area. (See also *Cambric*.)

BURLAP

A sturdy fabric woven from yarns made from the coarse fibers of jute or hemp, burlap is used to cover springs and to serve as a protective layer between them and the stuffing material (burlap was especially im-portant before foam rubber and its less expensive variations were com-monly marketed, when stuffing ma-terials were loose and could easily scatter between the spring coils).

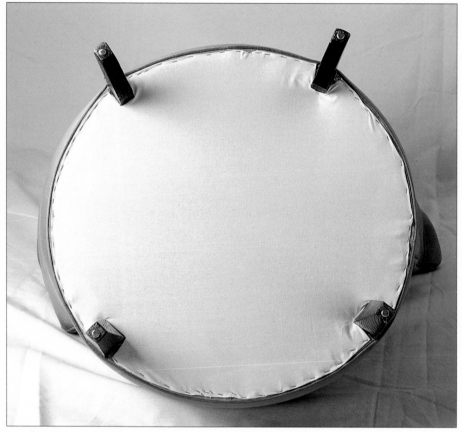

Muslin bottoming

Burlap is available in different weights and is used to cover springs.

Burlap is tacked to the furniture frame after the springs are tied, with its edges folded back to give double thickness beneath the tack heads. Available in different weights from 7.5 to 16 ounces (0.2 to 0.5kg), the burlap used on most mass-produced furnishings is 10 ounces (0.3kg), al-though a 12-ounce (0.4kg) weight is recommended for custom pieces when one can afford to pay for supe-rior strength.

CAMBRIC

A plain, usually black cotton fabric, cambric is the material stretched along the bottom of a furnishing as a dustcover.

COTTON FELT

Cotton spun into sheets, cotton felt is used as a pad over coarse stuff-ings and in between temporary and final covers.

Cotton felt is used as a topping over coarse stuffing or as a bridge between temporary and final cover.

Muslin is often used as a first covering before the final upholstery.

COTTON WEBBING

Not meant as a replacement for durable jute webbing, cotton webbing is used mainly for reinforcing the arms and backs of lighter upholstered pieces.

EXCELSIOR

A product made from basswood or poplar, excelsior is used as a foundation material on cheaper furniture, though it has poor resiliency.

JUTE WEBBING

Webbing in its traditional form refers to jute webbing—a sturdy, tightly woven tape made from stout jute fibers. Various widths are available, but the most common for commercial use is 3.5 inches (8.8cm). For custom upholstering, the wider and more expensive 4-inch (10cm) width is popular. A webbing's grade can be easily detected by the coloration of the stripes woven at its edges: the red stripe indicates highest quality, blue represents medium quality, and black identifies the least expensive.

MUSLIN

An inexpensive general utility fabric, muslin is used for temporary or first coverings that go beneath the outer upholstery cover. An inner cover of muslin (or possibly duck, durable, closely woven cotton fabric) is desired when the outer fabric is a pile, such as velour, or when the outer upholstery is a lightweight or low-grade leather. Muslin prevents the pile fabric covering from wearing loose after friction, and it reduces the friction that causes leather upholstery to stretch.

PAD

This material is the base on which the stuffing is placed before the entire upholstery treatment is covered with fabric, leather, or a synthetic material.

PLASTIC WEBBING

Water resistant, plastic webbing is used commonly for outdoor furniture. Available in all dimensions and colors, its one drawback is that it will eventually deteriorate when exposed to prolonged sunlight.

RUBBERIZED HAIR

Rubberized hog's hair (hog's hair that has been processed with rubber for greater strength) is often used for seat and back foundations on upholstered furnishings. After being processed, the hog's hair undergoes rigid tests for strength and resiliency.

Strips of webbing support the springs and ultimately the stuffing materials.

STEEL WEBBING

Usually restricted to less expensive upholstered seating pieces, steel webbing doesn't sag, but it also doesn't offer the comfort of jute webbing because it reduces a furnishing's resiliency. It is sold under different trade names (which often market the no-sag feature). For comfortable upholstered pieces, however, steel webbing is recommended for use only to reinforce a weak piece of jute webbing.

WADDING

A thin layer of cotton contained between two sheets of soft paper, this material is used like cotton felt, as a topping for coarse stuffings and as a bridge between temporary and final covers.

WEBBING

This is the material used as a base or platform for the upholstery springs and stuffing materials. Because it is the foundation material, it must be extremely strong to ensure maximum load-bearing for a comfortable seat over time.

GIMP

This is a fancy braid that is used to hide the edges of the upholstery covering where it meets the frame; it is also used to hide conspicuous or unsightly seams.

GIMP TACKS

Upholstery tacks with small, lacquered heads available in different colors, gimp tacks are used for upholstery work on places where the head of the tack is visible.

PINCERS

These pliers are used to extract small tacks and staples from furniture frames.

STITCHING TWINE

This flax or linen twine is used for stitching the springs to the webbing, the burlap to the springs, and the stuffing to the burlap. Sometimes referred to as mattress twine, it also is used in making spring edges and edge rolls.

TACKS

An essential item in traditional upholstering, tacks are available in a range of sizes and are put to a number of different uses. Standard upholsterers' tacks are used to attach fabrics; webbing tacks are used to hold webbing; gimp tacks are used for exposed areas; and fancy tacks nnare used as decorative trim, primarily on antiques. The rule of thumb in selecting tacks is that they be small enough not to split the timber of the furniture, yet large enough to hold the upholstery material is place so there is no danger of its pulling loose. Sizes range from $3/16$ inch (0.5cm) up to $15/16$ inch (2.4cm), with two shank sizes available in each length (shanks will be graded as either improved or fine, with improved referring to a thicker shank and larger head than their fine counterparts).

SPRING TWINE

This type of twine is used to tie spring seats into position. It features a polished or waxed finish and has the strength to preserve the life of the springs it holds. A good grade of hemp twine or a six-ply Italian hemp are the best choices.

Tacks serve many purposes in upholstery, including a decorative one on this leather club chair.

Buttons form the deep tufts on this sofa.

BIBLE FRONT

This indicates an upholstery treatment in which there is a bold rounded edge to front a seat.

BLIND STITCH

These stitches are formed with twine to consolidate the stuffing material.

BACK-TACKING

This method of attaching an upholstery covering to the frame conceals the tacking on the outside backs and arms with straight edges.

Backtacking conceals tacks.

BIAS CUTTING

A term especially important when following instructions for a do-it-yourself upholstery project, this refers to cutting the fabric on the diagonal, across the threads.

BRIDLE TIES

Another method of binding a filling, these are loops of twine that hold the materials in place.

BUTTONING

One of the most beautiful and elegant of upholstery treatments, this process forms deep diamond-shaped patterns in the covering through the indentations created from carefully placed buttons.

CHAMFER

An edge that is shaved or rounded, a chamfer is required when making a bevel on a corner of wood, or when joining two welts of leather.

FLOAT BUTTONING

This technique has buttons lightly pulled onto the covering, without deep, tufted grooves.

JOIN

This is the simple process of connecting two pieces of fabric with a machine-stitched seam.

LASHING

As the lacing and knotting together of spring coils with heavy twine, lashing prevents lateral movement of the springs.

MOCK CUSHION

An upholstery treatment that creates the appearance of a cushion where there is actually only a flat seat is known as a mock cushion.

PICKING

Hard-packed stuffing fibers require picking—separating and fluffing up—either by hand or by machine.

PULL-OVER EDGE

When a seat front edge is covered by pulling the material straight over it, it is called a pull-over edge.

Joining two pieces of fabric with a machine-stitched seam.

Cushions with firm fillings need to be picked or fluffed.

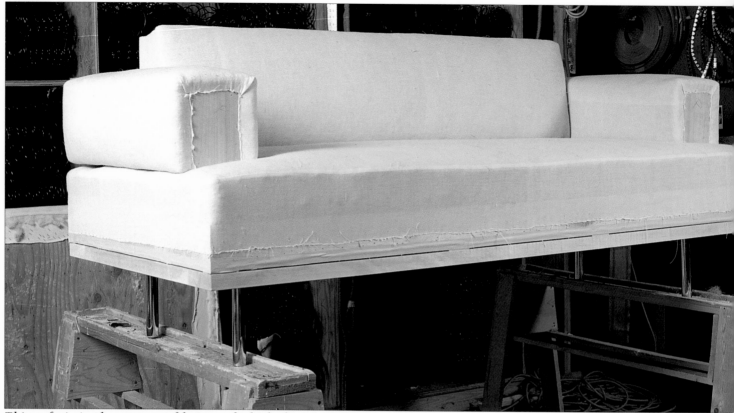

This sofa is in the process of being refurbished.

A chair undergoing ripping.

REFURBISHING

In terms of upholstery, refurbishing means repairing or renewing the original or existing treatment.

RIPPING

The removal of an upholstery covering or stuffing from the furniture frame is known as ripping.

ROLL EDGE

A commercially made roll purchased by the yard is used to create a roll edge that prevents stuffing from working away from the edge of the furniture frame.

RUCHES

These are the decorative trims that hide joins in coverings.

SPRING EDGE

This creates a flexible edge for seats or backs.

STITCHED EDGE

This padded edge is formed over the front of the spring burlap to create the desired final shape.

STUFFOVER CHAIR

This kind of chair is completely stuffed throughout and covered, with no exposed bare frame.

TACK ROLL

One method of making a soft edge on a timber frame is with a tack roll.

TOP STUFFING

This process (and its result) refers to interior upholstery when it is applied to the top surface of seat members only and not within the frame.

A tack roll gives this chair its soft edge.

CONCLUSION

IF YOU HAVE TAKEN THE TIME to carefully follow the instructions and study the information contained in this book, then by now you should feel confident that you understand your own tastes and lifestyle needs, and that you know how to translate these into appropriate choices of upholstery styles, materials, and techniques. In addition, you should be sufficiently informed that you are no longer intimidated by the complexity and variety with which you will be faced when you go to purchase or commission a work of upholstery. Congratulations! As an educated and savvy consumer, with a clear understanding of your needs and desires, you are now ready to enter into the no-longer-daunting process of selecting and purchasing a piece of upholstered furniture that will be sure to give you many years of comfort and contentment.

Above: Upholstered furnishings are enjoyed in every room of the home today—even the bedroom.

Right: Creating a beautiful home that reflects your personal style is well within reach. Enjoy the process and you'll enjoy the results for years to come.

SUGGESTED READING

Bishop, Robert, and Patricia Coblentz. *American Decorative Arts*. New York: Harry N. Abrams, 1982.

Brumstead, Elaine. *The Home Sewing Library's Soft Furnishings*. London: Dorling Kindersley Ltd., 1987.

Cargill, Katrin. *The Soft Furnishing Book*. London: Reed Consumer Books Ltd., 1994.

Colvin, Maggie. *Pure Fabrication*. Radnor, PA.: Chilton Book Co., 1985.

Emery, Marc. *Furniture By Architects*. New York: Harry N. Abrams, 1983.

Fabbro, Mario Dal. *Upholstered Furniture: Design and Construction*. New York: McGraw-Hill, 1969.

Gates, Dorothy, et al. *The Complete Book of Soft Furnishings*. London: Ward Lock, 1989.

Gottshall, Franklin H. *Heirloom Furniture*. Milwaukee: The Bruce Publishing Co., 1957.

Marshall, Mel. *How to Repair, Reupholster, and Refinish Furniture*. New York: Harper & Row, 1979.

McDonald, Robert J. *Basic Upholstery Repair and Restoration*. London: B. T. Batsford, Ltd., 1984.

————. *Upholstery Repair and Restoration*. New York: Charles Scribner's Sons, 1977.

Peverill, Sue. *The Fabric Decorator*. London: MacDonald & Co. Ltd., 1988.

Singer's More Sewing For the Home. Minnetonka, Minn.: Cy De Cosse Inc., 1987.

Tierney, William F. *Modern Upholstering Methods*. McKnight & McKnight Publishing, 1965.

Torelli, Michael E., and Ellen K. Haggerty. *Reupholstering For the Home Craftsman*. Radnor, PA.: Chilton Book Co., 1977.

PHOTOGRAPHY CREDITS

Archive Photos: 29

Art Resource: Bridgeman: 19, 23, 24, 25, 34 both; Victoria & Albert Museum, London: 17 bottom, 18 right

Courtesy Avery Boardman: ©Frank Ritter: 16-17

Corbis-Bettmann: 12, 28, 30 left, 35, 42, 144

©Manuel Canovas: 75, 133 top

©Grey Crawford: 76, 126; 52, 53, 62, 79 (designed by Charles Riley); 86 (designed by Lori Erenberg)

©Derrick & Love: 32 (designed by Alvin Schneider); 139

Courtesy DesignTex: 55, 130, 132 both, 133 bottom left, 134 bottom, 135 all, 136 top, 137 top left and right, 138 both, 141 bottom; 131 top right and bottom, 133 bottom right, 140 (One Plus One division)

©Phillip H. Ennis: 95 (designed by Richard L. Ridge); 112 (designed by Stephen and Gail Huberman)

©e.t.archive: 14, 15, 74

©Feliciano: 77; 18 left, 73 (Safa fabric designed by Fonthill Ltd.)

©Nancy Hill: 5, 6, 123 bottom; 36 bottom (designed by Anne Mullin Interiors); 2, 60-61, 67, 111 (designed by Karyne Johnson of Panache Interiors); 91, 96, 99 (designed by Jan Burket Interior Design)

©image/dennis krukowski: 1,124-125; 8 (designed by Robert E. Tartarini Interiors); 43 (designed by Mariette Himes Gomes); 68 left (designed by Peter Moore); 87 (designed by Aubergine Interiors Ltd.); 94 (designed by Charles Krewson Interior Design); 97 (designed by Anne Eisenhower Inc.); 105 (designed by Gary Crain Associates Inc.); 106 left (designed by Lemeau & Llana Inc.); 109, 119 right (designed by Vincente Wolf); 110 (designed by Walker & Associates, Inc.); 113 (designed by Lincoln Interiors Inc.); 117 (designed by David Eugene Bell, A.S.I.D.); 151 bottom (designed by Melvin Dwork Inc.)

Courtesy The Knoll Group: 51 top, 56, 57 all, 58 left, 59 top, 102, 127 right, 134 top

©Samantha Larrance: 36 top

©Peter Paige: 40

©Robert Perron: 41

©David Phelps: 44, 45, 46, 47, 48, 49, 51 bottom, 68-69, 78 both, 81, 82, 83, 88, 89,108 (courtesy American Homestyle & Gardening); 59 bottom, 64, 65, 66 (courtesy Ladies Home Journal); 70, 71, 72 (designed by Charles Riley); 90 (designed by Stanley Hura/First For Women); 103, 106-107 (designed by Jeffrey Hitchcock); 104 (courtesy Gregarious/Pineo); 114-115, 122 bottom, 123 top, 128-129, 154-155 (designed by Linda Chase); 118-119 (courtesy First For Women); 136 bottom, 137 bottom (designed by Lorraine Forenza Henry/courtesy First For Women); 142 (fabric designed by Sabina Fay Braxton); 143, 145, 146 both, 147 both, 148, 150 both, 151 top, 152 both, 153, 154 left

(designed by Michael Berman/courtesy American Homestyle & Gardening)

©Paul Rocheleau: 13, 63

©Eric Roth: 9 (designed by Charles Spada); 37 (designed by Carole Kaplan of Two By Two Interior Design); 38-39, 50, 98 (designed by Peter J. Wheeler Associates); 80 (photographed at Adair Country Inn); 84-85, 100 (designed by Francoise Theise of Adesso Furniture); 92 (designed by Peter Lawton of Design Plus); 93 (Andrew Reczkowski interior designer for Bloomingdale's); 101 (designed by Cann & Company); 116 (designed by Julie Alvarez de Toledo); 120 left (designed by C&J Katz Studio); 120-121 (designed by Brad Morash); 122 top, 141 top (photographed at the Beauport Museum); 149 (styled by Gwen Simpkins)

Courtesy Schumacher: 54, 58 right, 127 left, 131 top left

Courtesy Smith & Watson: 20 left, 26, 27

©Superstock: 10-11, 20-21, 22, 30 right, 31 both, 33

INDEX